Why Aren't You
Your Own Boss?

Other Books by Paul and Sarah Edwards

The Best Home Businesses for the 21st Century

Changing Directions Without Losing Your Way

Cool Careers for Dummies*

The Entrepreneurial Parent*

Finding Your Perfect Work

Getting Business to Come to You*

Home Businesses You Can Buy*

Home-Based Business for Dummies*

Making Money in Cyberspace*

Making Money with Your Computer at Home

The Practical Dreamer's Handbook

Secrets of Self-Employment

Teaming Up: The Small Business Guide to Collaborating with Others to Boost Your Earnings and Expand Your Horizons*

Working from Home

Other Books by Peter Economy

The Complete MBA for Dummies

Consulting for Dummies*

Home-Based Business for Dummies*

Leadership Ensemble: Lessons in Collaborative Management from the World's Only Conductorless Orchestra*

Managing for Dummies*

Raising Capital for Dummies*

*With coauthors

P A U L   E D W A R D S
S A R A H   E D W A R D S
P E T E R   E C O N O M Y

Why Aren't You Your Own Boss?

*Leaping Over the Obstacles
That Stand Between
You and Your Dream*

P R I M A   P U B L I S H I N G

Published by Prima Publishing, Roseville, California. Member of the Crown Publishing Group, a division of Random House, Inc., New York.

PRIMA PUBLISHING and colophon are trademarks of Random House, Inc., registered with the United States Patent and Trademark Office.

Library of Congress Cataloging-in-Publication Data
Edwards, Paul.
   Why aren't you your own boss? : leaping over the obstacles that stand between you and your dream / Paul Edwards, Sarah Edwards, and Peter Economy. —1st ed.
      p.   cm.
   Includes index.
   ISBN 0-7615-1537-2
   1. New business enterprises—Management. 2. Small business—Management. 3. Self-employed. I. Edwards, Sarah (Sarah A.).
II. Economy, Peter. III. Title.
HD62.5 .E385   2003
658.1'141—dc21   2002155296

03 04 05 06 07 HH 10 9 8 7 6 5 4 3 2 1
Printed in the United States of America

First Edition

Visit us online at www.primapublishing.com

This book is dedicated to the aspirations of the millions of people who each year say "If only I could be my own boss" because they're not earning what they're worth; are locked into dead-end, unsatisfying jobs; would rather be doing something else during their working hours; don't want to be holding the job they now do for twenty years; don't believe their job will last twenty years or until retirement; would not recommend their job to their children; or aren't where they wanted or expected to be at this time in their lives. We have met you over the years and dedicate this book to helping those of you who wish so much but need just the right tip or the right resource to move on with your dreams.

If this book doesn't provide an answer for what's holding you back, the authors will consider your situation individually and do their best to provide suggestions. Contact "Ask Paul and Sarah" at www.workingfromhome.com.

CONTENTS

ACKNOWLEDGMENTS

We give our sincere thanks to the publishing staff at Prima, including Shawn Vreeland, Matt Jarrette, JoAnne White, Jennifer Risden, Brenda Ginty, Alice Feinstein, and particularly our editor, Jennifer Sander. We thank our agents, Bob Diforio, Marilyn Allen, and Colleen O'Shea of the D4EO Literary Agency.

We acknowledge Kristie Tamsevicius of webmomz.com for encouraging users of her site to participate in a survey that helped us verify barriers people face in becoming their own boss.

Paul and Sarah thank Peter Economy for his commitment to this project.

Peter thanks Paul and Sarah for the opportunity to work with them again.

CHAPTER ONE

What's Holding You Back?

Why aren't you your own boss?

In the more than two decades since we pioneered the field of home-based business, we have interviewed, spoken to, worked with, and had the privilege of meeting thousands of men and women across the nation, each one of whom shared something in common: a burning desire to be his or her own boss. The facts bear this out. Seven in ten Americans at some time in their lives want to be their own boss, to own their own business—taking control of their lives and their futures.

And, for many of these thousands of people, that's exactly what has happened. They have quit their jobs to follow their dreams, leaving behind the security of a regular paycheck and a cushy benefits package with an established company. They are among the more than twenty-two million small businesses in the United States responsible for creating two out of three new jobs in the economy—most of which were started by people just like you who decided to become their own boss.

But, for every person we've met who has become his or her own boss, there are many more who, for one reason or another, never make the desired leap to independence. Research studies report that, while one in every twenty-five American adults is making an effort to start his or her own business in any given year—some seven million efforts a year—fewer than half get under way. That leaves a lot of people who get stuck on the way to achieving their dreams.

> Seven in ten Americans at some time in their lives want to be their own boss, to own their own business—taking control of their lives and their futures.

You'd like to be one of those at least, right? But . . . there's a "but," isn't there? Maybe a whole lot of buts. What if you could get past those buts and really make something happen? That's what this book is all about—it's about getting past the buts, without your having to change who you are or your values or intentions, turning your dreams into reality.

We have long been fascinated by the question of what it is that causes so many people—people who have a very strong desire to be their own boss—to falter on the path to an independent career. Is there something within successful entrepreneurs that others lack—some trait, some skill, or simply some good fortune?

We don't think so. We've known people who are successfully self-employed with all types of personalities, including shyness, introversion, and modesty. We've met people whose voices are so soft they're difficult to hear over the telephone. We've even known individuals who have created businesses while confined to a bed, flat on their backs. We're not referring to superstar motivational speakers who have overcome such great handicaps that it makes all of us wonder what they have that we don't. We mean everyday, ordinary individuals with a desire and commitment to a better way of life. Before the twentieth century, most Americans were self-employed, as farmers, craftsmen, and tradespeople.

So what's the missing piece to your puzzle? What barriers are preventing you from being your own boss? What are the obvious ones as well as the less obvious ones? Most important, what can you do to overcome them? We believe you can find the answers and the strategies you need in the chapters that follow.

BE YOUR OWN BOSS PROFILE

I want so badly to start my own business. The problem is that I have no idea what it is I want to do. How do I find my niche? I want to do something that is flexible and will not exclude my children. I have an associate's degree in office management and have been working in a nursing home. I work very well with people. I am full of information. People are always asking me where they go for this or that. If I don't know, I always know how to find out. For example, if someone is having trouble with their landlord, I know where to go for help. If someone is having financial problems, I know who can help. In staff meetings at work, people always come to me afterward and ask questions, even though they heard the exact same thing I did and I don't know any more than they do. They just know that I know how to find the answers. I also love to read. I love computers. I'm not looking to get rich. I would never want to put in the time that Bill Gates does to get his money. I only want to make enough money to live comfortably and be happy. I just don't know where to go from here.

What's Holding You Back?

Many reasons explain why people put their dreams on the back burner, but from the thousands of aspiring entrepreneurs we've encountered—listening to or reading about their dreams, their successes, and their failures—we've narrowed these reasons down into seven key categories:

- *I don't know the first step to take.* Many people know that they want to be their own boss, but they literally do not have the first clue about how to get started. Many of these same people don't even know what kind of business they want to start or whether a particular business really makes financial sense for them.

- *I know what I need to do, but just can't get myself going.* Of course, many people with dreams to become their own boss know exactly what kind of business they want to start and

---

BE YOUR OWN BOSS PROFILE

I've been mulling over a home business for three (count 'em, three) years. Currently I am a stay-at-home mom. I've done some market research, written an informal business plan, named my business . . . but I'm stalled. I haven't gotten a business license or done any advertising. I have most of the equipment I need, but I balk when it comes to plunking down the money needed to officially start up the business. I want to incorporate so that my business and personal finances will remain completely separate and my personal liability will be reduced, which will cost about $1,000 initially, with maintenance fees every year thereafter. Does there come a point where you just have to jump in with two feet and say, "Okay, this is it! I am starting!"?

BE YOUR OWN BOSS PROFILE

I am in a desperate position. I need a way to make money and be able to stay home. I lost my job in January, and my hubby has just started a new job. We were living on the edge for a while and then got ahead for a little bit, but then I had some medical issues and no insurance to help pay the bills. A week ago my husband got hurt and was out of work for three days and that has put us under, literally. I have *absolutely no money* to put up for a start-up fee or to start a new business. I don't mean to tell you this to feel sorry for me, but it is the cold, hard truth. Now a little about myself: I have been making my own greeting cards for about two and a half years.

---

what they should do. They have been dreaming and planning for a long time, waiting for an opportunity to break loose. The problem is, they keep waiting, and waiting, and the opportunity they so long for never does come along.

- *I don't have enough money.* This is the traditional stumbling block for many people who want to start their own

---

BE YOUR OWN BOSS PROFILE

I have a home business idea; I have a name; I have written out an informal business plan; I have started on a letterhead and on a business card idea. I even had multiple voice mail boxes put on my telephone. However, I have not gone to register with the county and acquire a DBA ("doing business as" or fictitious name registration). Is that necessary before I begin, or is it too soon for that? What step do I take next? Am I on the right track?

> ## BE YOUR OWN BOSS PROFILE
>
> I have to admit—I am a little scared. I enjoy cooking, and it is amazing to see people's eyes light up when I tell them that I am an aspiring personal chef. I would like this eventually to become something I can do into retirement. I have lots of things I enjoy doing, but . . .
>
> Am I being a big chicken? I have this dream that my little business will start out very small and grow neatly in gradual, manageable steps. Is this just silly, or is there a way to achieve that? I guess what I want to know is, Is it normal to be afraid to take that final step in starting a business? How did you overcome that and go on to be the raging successes that I know you all are? I am trying to overcome my fears.

businesses, and it is also one of the most common reasons for the failure of established businesses. As the old saying goes, "It takes money to make money," and not having the money available to invest in your new business seems like a formidable obstacle on the road to success.

- *I don't know anything about business.* While most of us work or have worked for a business at one time or another in our lives, relatively few of us have actually started and run our own businesses from scratch. The fact is, starting up and running a business is a very different proposition than simply working for one, and not knowing the ins and outs of business can make starting one of your own seem quite intimidating.

- *I have hang-ups.* It takes a lot of courage to make the decision to start your own business—especially when doing so means exchanging a comfortable job or career for an uncertain future. Lack of confidence, lack of expertise, fear of success, depression—all of these things and more

---

BE YOUR OWN BOSS PROFILE

I need some advice. Let me fill you in. I am a mother of a darling four-year-old girl. I currently work full-time doing something that I do not enjoy. My talents are somewhere along the lines of crafting, selling, and writing. But my husband owns his own business, and there are some issues regarding *his* taxes. So I'm afraid that if I quit my job, I am going to sink my family into poverty. I'm not the only one who isn't sure if this is feasible. Most of my relatives, particularly my in-laws and my dad, think it's crazy for me to quit this job. But I hate it there. *Help!*

---

can hang you up and turn you away from your dreams, no matter how much you want to achieve them.

- *I have problems.* Okay. So we've all got problems. Only one thing: Some people's problems are bigger than other people's problems. Whether it's lack of support from family, friends, and spouse, or physical incapabilities, or being too old or too young, or any number of other afflictions, imagined or real, all of these problems can delay or even permanently defer the move to starting your own business.

BE YOUR OWN BOSS PROFILE

I have looked at The Pampered Chef and other companies. I don't have very good people skills and am scared to death to start something new. Also, I have no friends to start selling to. My hobbies now include crafting and surfing the net for ideas to make money. I have taken on a few of them, but I don't follow through on any one of them.

- *I have a hard time following through.* This, of course, might very well be the greatest hurdle for anyone who hopes to be his or her own boss. No matter how many of the other obstacles you face and conquer, if you are unable to follow your quest to completion, then you'll never achieve your dreams of self-employment. The lack of a "completion gene" (you'll find a complete explanation of this critical ingredient for success in business in chapter 9) can doom even the best ideas or the most sincerely aspiring entrepreneurs.

You know that buts like these are very real obstacles in your path; if they weren't, you would already be your own boss. You also know that most things of value in life present certain obstacles to overcome. The big question is this: How do you realistically get past the obstacles you face right now? The first step is to identify and later to develop strategies to deal with and overcome the obstacles that you face. Let's start with you.

Is BYOBing Really for You?

We're obviously big believers in the power of being your own boss (BYOB). We believe that being your own boss can be the key to unlocking your full potential and bringing you true happiness and fulfillment. Not only have we met thousands of people who have successfully taken charge of their own work lives—people who now find it difficult to imagine ever working for someone else again—but we ourselves have made the transition to becoming our own bosses.

But just as some people prefer mountains to seashores, some of us are more comfortable in the world of steady paychecks and other people's rules. We're not going to pretend that everyone is cut out for self-employment. Some people are clearly meant to be entrepreneurs—to be their own bosses—

INDEPENDENT CAREER QUOTIENT (EQ) TEST

I am persistent.	YES	MAYBE	NO
When I'm interested in a project, I need less sleep.	YES	MAYBE	NO
When there's something I want, I keep my goal clearly in mind.	YES	MAYBE	NO
I like to examine mistakes, and I learn from them.	YES	MAYBE	NO
I like to make and keep New Year's resolutions.	YES	MAYBE	NO
I have a strong personal need to succeed.	YES	MAYBE	NO
I have lots of new and different ideas.	YES	MAYBE	NO
I am comfortable adapting to changing circumstances.	YES	MAYBE	NO
I am curious.	YES	MAYBE	NO
I am intuitive.	YES	MAYBE	NO
If something can't be done, I find a way.	YES	MAYBE	NO
I see problems as challenges.	YES	MAYBE	NO
I like taking calculated chances.	YES	MAYBE	NO
I'll gamble on a good idea, even if it isn't a sure thing.	YES	MAYBE	NO
To learn something new, I will explore unfamiliar subjects.	YES	MAYBE	NO
I can recover from emotional setbacks.	YES	MAYBE	NO
I feel sure of myself to travel into unfamiliar territory.	YES	MAYBE	NO
I'm a positive person, even when things are challenging.	YES	MAYBE	NO
I like to experiment with new ways to do things.	YES	MAYBE	NO
I don't mind undergoing sacrifices to attain possible long-term rewards.	YES	MAYBE	NO
I like to do things my own way.	YES	MAYBE	NO
I don't mind having the buck stop with me.	YES	MAYBE	NO
I don't mind being alone.	YES	MAYBE	NO
I like to be in control.	YES	MAYBE	NO
I have a reputation for being stubborn.	YES	MAYBE	NO

and some people are clearly meant to work for someone else. That's okay. The most important thing is finding a career that enables you to feel your time in this life is well spent, whether you are the boss or are working for someone else.

Some people think they want to be their own boss, but the closer they get to doing it, they find it's not as attractive as they thought. You might describe this as a "closer-you-get-to-the-sun-the-hotter it is" phenomenon, but the fact is heat—that's a burning passion for being on your own—is one of the most important elements of being successfully self-employed.

How about you? Is this really for you? We offer the test on page 9, adapted from one the Small Business Administration (SBA) offers on its Web site (www.sba.gov) to help you decide if you would find running your own business as attractive as you think. Take a few minutes right now to see what it says about you.

What do you think? For each yes answer, give yourself three points; for each maybe, two points; for each no, zero points. Total up your score and see what it suggests.

Number of yes answers: _____ × 3 = _____
Number of maybe answers: _____ × 2 = _____
Your total: _____

- If you scored between 60 and 75, being your own boss will probably be as attractive to you as you expect.
- If you scored between 48 and 59, you are attracted to being your own boss but may need to push and nudge yourself along to bring certain aspects of your personality to the fore and develop them more fully. Alternatively, you may want to consider hiring someone to help you with the areas that aren't suited to you.
- If you scored between 37 and 47, you may not find operating a business on your own as attractive as you thought,

so you might want to look for a business partner who can complement you in the areas you're not attracted to.

- If you scored below 37, self-employment may not be for you. You may be happier and more successful working for someone else. Of course, only you can make that decision. But before you go any further, look deep within yourself. Do you really want to start your own business? Are you sure that's who you are? Do you really want to leave the comfort of your job with its benefits and steady paychecks, or is this something you think you should do or a pleasant panacea you fantasize about after a rough day?

You Know Yourself Better Than We Do

The fact is, you know yourself better than anyone else does. You know what you can and can't do, you know your personal limits—from the heights of your greatest dreams to the depths of your darkest insecurities—and you know the boundaries of your own personal zone of comfort. It's up to you to decide when you should make the move to becoming your own boss. Our job is to help you

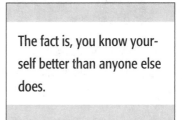

The fact is, you know yourself better than anyone else does.

identify the obstacles that may have gotten in your way—obstacles that you may not be aware of or not know what to do about—and to provide you with strategies for moving them out of the way.

So let's get started!

THE WHY AREN'T YOU YOUR OWN BOSS OBSTACLE QUIZ

As we have seen, there are many different reasons that prevent people from becoming their own boss. The problem is identifying (1) where you are stuck and (2) exactly why? The answers to the twenty-four simple yes-or-no questions that follow will help you pinpoint just how stuck or unstuck you really are and where. Give yourself one point for every yes answer and zero points for every no answer. After you finish the quiz, total up the results and check them against the scoring guide.

1. Do you spend more time planning than you spend doing? Yes ❏ No ❏

2. Do you often find yourself daydreaming when you are at work? Yes ❏ No ❏

3. Are you worrying more than taking action? Yes ❏ No ❏

4. Are you afraid that you're too young (or too old) to be a success? Yes ❏ No ❏

5. Do you put off dealing with important issues that threaten to derail your career, finances, or relationships? Yes ❏ No ❏

6. Do you feel that it's necessary to learn as much as possible about starting and running a business before you actually dive in? Yes ❏ No ❏

7. Are you only a paycheck or two away from financial disaster? Yes ❏ No ❏

8. Do you have a hard time following through on projects and bringing them to completion? Yes ❏ No ❏

9. Do you feel certain that you want to start your own business, but you are totally lost when it comes to figuring out what kind of business to start and how you'll go about starting it?   Yes ❑   No ❑

10. Are you uncomfortably nervous that you know very little about running a business?   Yes ❑   No ❑

11. Do you have problems working with people?   Yes ❑   No ❑

12. Do you put off doing what you need to do until a crisis develops?   Yes ❑   No ❑

13. Do you put off doing tasks until you feel that you can do them perfectly?   Yes ❑   No ❑

14. Does the fear of change paralyze your efforts to achieve your dreams?   Yes ❑   No ❑

15. Do you obsess about things you would like to do but rarely get around to doing?   Yes ❑   No ❑

16. Are you overwhelmed by all the possibilities when you think about the kind of business to start?   Yes ❑   No ❑

17. Do you commit yourself to doing so many things that you can't find time to do a thorough job on any one of them?   Yes ❑   No ❑

18. Is doing something prestigious that commands respect more important to you than possible higher earnings or doing things your own way?   Yes ❑   No ❑

(continues)

(continued)

19. Do other priorities keep getting in the way of your
    plans for success?   Yes ❏   No ❏

20. Do the hurdles to making a positive change in your
    life seem increasingly insurmountable the closer
    you get to them?   Yes ❏   No ❏

21. Is it hard for you to make decisions and then to
    stick with them once you do?   Yes ❏   No ❏

22. Are your plans to start your own business on hold
    because you lack the funds necessary to make a
    go of it?   Yes ❏   No ❏

23. Are you worried that you might pick a business
    and fail, or that you might pick the wrong business
    and it might succeed?   Yes ❏   No ❏

24. Do key people in your life (spouse, family, friends)
    pooh-pooh your desire to start your own business
    or even oppose you?   Yes ❏   No ❏

Scoring: How Stuck Are You?

As we said, give yourself one point for every yes answer and zero
points for every no answer. Now add up all your answers to get your
total for this quiz, and let's see how you did.

Number of yes answers:	_____ × 1 =	_____
Number of no answers:	_____ × 0 =	_____
Your total:		_____

0–8 points: Not So Stuck! This may surprise you, but you're actually not very stuck at all. Sure, you might have a couple of minor obstacles, but with some ideas about the particulars and a slight nudge in the right direction, you'll be on your way.

9–16 points: A Little Stuck! It looks like you're conflicted about the changes you'll need to make in your life to achieve your dreams. While there are as many good reasons in your mind for making a major change in your life, there are reasons against it, too. With a little help, you can focus on the positive—on the success you know you can achieve if you put your mind to it—and worry less about the negatives. Use this book to help you do your research, to deal with the obstacles on your path in a concerted and methodical way.

17–24 points: Pretty Stuck! As you have probably already noticed, you often become overwhelmed by the many different issues starting out on your own presents. Unfortunately, you are also feeling resistant—even afraid—to change. Use this book to begin, taking small steps, one by one, around the obstacles to your dreams. As you achieve smaller goals, you can build on your success.

So, how stuck are you? While this quiz provides you with a general idea of where you stand, your particular answers to the quiz can serve as a compass to how to overcome the obstacles you need to address before you'll be able to proceed.

Using This Book as Your Compass

Now that you've identified the specifics of what's getting between you and your dreams of self-employment, you may be wondering whether you'll ever get past these obstacles. They're probably not a big surprise to you, right?

It's our belief that if you truly want to get past these obstacles, you can. So take a look at any questions in The Why Aren't You Your Own Boss Quiz that you answered yes, then on the following chart find the chapter that addresses these issues. Once you find the chapters that address the obstacles

IF YOU ANSWERED YES TO QUESTIONS	GO TO CHAPTER
9	Chapter 2: Not Knowing the First Step to Take
1, 2, 5, 12, 15, 20, or 21	Chapter 3: I Know What I Need to Do, but I Just Can't Get Myself Going!
7 or 22	Chapter 4: But I Don't Have the Money!
6 or 10	Chapter 5: I Don't Know the Nitty-Gritty of Starting a Business
3, 11, 13, 14, 16, 18, 19, or 23	Chapter 6: All Talk, No Action: Is It Me? Do I Have Hang-Ups! Part I
	AND
	Chapter 7: All Talk, No Action: Is It Me? Do I Have Hang-Ups! Part II
4 or 24	Chapter 8: But My Problems Are Real!
8 or 17	Chapter 9: The Single Most Important Ingredient

that you personally face, you can turn directly to those chapters and start working there.

At the end of each chapter, you'll be asked to list three things you want or need to do to start your business and to write them down in the Personal Action Plan in Appendix A: Take-Off Section beginning on page 294. Together all the tasks you identify will comprise your personal action plan, which you begin implementing before you finish this book.

Also as you read through each chapter, you'll discover resources you didn't know existed, strategies you never thought of, and solutions you wouldn't have imagined—culled from the success stories of thousands of people like yourself, people who were asking the same question you've been asking: Why aren't I my own boss? They faced the same obstacles and found the answers, and so can you.

As you work through the chapters, you'll be surprised with the shift in your attitude about your chances for actually becoming your own boss. It will seem less like an impossible dream you must relegate to "maybe someday" and more like a realistic possibility. And that will only be the beginning. You'll actually be on your way to being your own boss. With each chapter, you'll be closer and closer until there are no more buts.

CHAPTER TWO

Not Knowing the First Step to Take

I've decided to start a business—what kind of business should I start?

I would like to work at home—how do I get started?

I don't have any money—how can I get a business going?

No matter what country they live in, or what line of work they do, or how rich or how poor they might be, almost everyone dreams of one thing: being their own boss. As a matter of fact, studies confirm that seven out of ten Americans at some time in their lives want to be their own boss, own their own businesses, and take control over their lives and their futures.

Many people (including you?) are so excited by the possibility of taking charge of their lives and leaving the 9-to-5 world of their careers behind that they actually decide to do more than just *dream* about it. They decide to *do* something about it. As we mentioned in the first chapter, every year more than seven million American adults make the decision to become their own bosses by starting their own businesses. That's a lot of people!

The only problem is, while these aspiring entrepreneurs are all bound and determined to walk down the path to personal independence—and they know exactly what kind of business they want to start—many of them have no idea of where the path to their dreams starts or how to get on it. Still others don't even know what kind of business they want to start, much less how to start it.

> Every year more than seven million American adults make the decision to become their own bosses by starting their own businesses.

If not knowing the first step to take or what business you should start is getting in the way of your dreams of independence, here's what you can do right now. Don't allow this critical phase of becoming your own boss continue to be a mystery. Step around this obstacle by asking the following questions:

Question 1: What kind of business should I start?

Question 2: Who will pay me to do what I want to do?

Question 3: How can I start with what I've got?

Let's go through these questions in detail. By the time you're done with this chapter, you'll know what kind of business you can start or be on the way to finding it, and you'll also know the best places to look for information on taking your first steps. Not only that, but you'll find out who will pay you to do what you want to do. You should be well on your way to leaping over this particular barrier and on the path to making your dreams of independence a reality.

A COUPON FOR SUCCESS

Many people know that they want to start a business but, when it comes right down to it, they really don't know what kind of business to start. Laurie Bebout, founder of Precision Advertising Distribution in Paducah, Kentucky, got the idea for her business in a moment of frustration over the fact that she had to buy a newspaper to receive money-saving coupons for local businesses. She thought, "Why can't I receive these coupons in the mail without buying a newspaper?" But instead of simply wondering why, Laurie took action—discovering a business need just waiting to be filled.

Knowing nothing about the advertising business (she already had a comfortable career as a nuclear safety engineer), Laurie used her computer and the Internet to learn more. She found the Web sites of companies that did deliver ads to people's doors, and she learned how these businesses worked. She also learned one piece of information that was particularly important: There was no company providing advertising directly to the residents of Paducah—the market was wide open for whatever company decided to step in. At that moment, Laurie resolved to start up her own business to deliver ads and coupons directly to consumers in their own homes.

Branching out from her initial research on the Internet, Laurie began to network with friends and businesspeople in her community. Potential customers convinced her that there was a very real need for her service, and she learned that she was eligible for a special $50,000 start-up loan available for new Paducah-based businesses. Not only that, but Laurie found out that, if she joined the local chamber of commerce, she would receive $1,000 in free advertising. Armed with all of this information and the many contacts she made in her community, Laurie completed a business plan, secured financing for her business, and hired four employees. Says Laurie, "Being my own boss is the best thing in the world."

Question 1: What Kind of Business Should I Start?

What kind of business *should* you start? If uncertainty about the answer to this question is stopping you from moving closer to your dreams of independence, then the very first thing you'll need to do is to decide what kind of business is right for you. And it *is* important to find the right answer to this question. If you find yourself bouncing from business idea to business idea, without settling on one that is best for you, then you'll be hard-pressed to focus enough of your energy on any one idea for long enough to get it off the ground. And focus is what it's all about when it comes to starting a successful business of your own.

Right about now, we suspect you're feeling just a bit like a kid in a candy store. There are so many delectable items to choose from that it's hard to decide on just one to buy and take home with you. Should you go for the big lollipop or maybe a handful of jelly beans? Or how about one of those candy apples or a nice piece of peanut brittle? When you're thinking about starting your own business, the sky is quite literally the limit—you can start any business you want. Perhaps you've always dreamed of having your own clothing boutique downtown, or maybe you've longed to leave the corporate world behind and start a home-based consulting practice for your field or industry. You may have decided that buying, rehabbing, and selling houses is just the ticket or that there is a gift basket business in your future. The possibilities are just about endless.

When Michael Reagan was searching for the right idea for a business of his own, he had no idea what kind of business he wanted to start. To come up with an answer, Reagan set aside six months to research a variety of different options. Says Reagan, "Every time a thought came to me about the charac-

---

WHAT WOMEN WANT

When people can't find what they want in their regular jobs, that often becomes a very strong motivation for them to strike out on their own. According to a Roper-Starch survey reported in *USA Today* in 2002, here's what women really want:

- 33 percent want equal pay. (As a business owner, you set your own salary and the opportunity is as small or as large as you are willing to work for.)
- 20 percent want more affordable health care. (With costs increasingly shifting to employees and deductibility of health insurance for sole proprietorships rising from 60 percent to 100 percent during the decade, regular employees are losing this advantage.)
- 15 percent want more flexibility at work. (When you own your own business, you're in charge!)
- 11 percent want more equal chores between spouses. (Increasingly, men are becoming employees of businesses their wives start.)
- 8 percent want more affordable day care. (Reduce it to zero, or make less expensive arrangements by working at home.)
- 8 percent want a four-day work week. (That's easy. How about half days?)

---

teristics of a business I would like to have, I wrote it down on a piece of paper." Eventually, Reagan's list numbered 103 different characteristics—things that he wanted and didn't want his business to be. "I didn't want consumer goods with inventory stacked on the shelf. I didn't want anything that was perishable. I didn't want anything that people could get sick from. I wanted something that is not just limited to a neighborhood, like a dry cleaner or pizza shop. I wanted something that was part of a service that will be purchased by business executives. I wanted something that was technology driven."

Reagan next began to match different kinds of businesses against his 103 characteristics. The final match? A sign company franchise. Reagan is very happy with his business, and he offers this advice to would-be entrepreneurs: "Learn a lot about yourself as a person as far as what you really should be doing as a profession for the rest of your life. And don't just get something because somebody tells you that it is a hot opportunity or a great deal or that you can make a lot of money."

> To avoid forever bouncing from idea to idea, never sure exactly which way to go or how to get there, you've got to find your focus.

If you're in the situation where you haven't decided what to do, this can be a major barrier in your path to personal independence. To get past this barrier—and we're certain you will—you've got to focus 100 percent of your efforts on finding the right path for you that will take you to your ultimate goal. Remember: To avoid forever bouncing from idea to idea, never sure exactly which way to go or how to get there, you've got to find your focus.

Once you decide what to do—and once you narrow your focus down to a single path—you'll be well on the way to surmounting the obstacle of not knowing where to start, and you'll be that much closer to turning your dreams into reality. The key to accomplishing this goal is to narrow down all of these many different possibilities into the one kind of work that (1) you're most passionate about and (2) offers the best money-making potential for you.

According to the Small Business Administration, basic ideas for your business most often come from the following sources:

A spin-off from your present occupation

A hobby or special interest

An answer to the question "Why isn't there a . . . ?"

A shortcoming in the products or services of others

A new or different way of using ordinary things

An observed need

A technological advance or changes in society or social customs

When Sylvie Charrier of Ottawa, Ontario, first started her business, she was a single mom with three kids who had no other means of support. While she knew that she wanted to be able to work from home, she really didn't know what kind of work she would do. In addition to these challenges:

- Sylvie didn't have a computer, and she didn't know how to use one anyway.
- Her typing rate was less than thirty words per minute.
- Her market was limited because she didn't speak French.

But, instead of dwelling on what she *couldn't* do (and, no doubt, there were many things Sylvie couldn't do), she sat down and made a list of everything she *could* do. To avoid pushing her business into some sort of preconceived niche, Sylvie picked a generic business name that could be used for most any sort of business she eventually settled on. She then created a flyer and a cover letter of introduction and made as

IMAGINING THE IDEAL

To get in touch with what you really want to do, it may be necessary to take some time to look deep within yourself and listen to what your heart tells you. One of the best ways to do this is to find a quiet space where you can sit down and relax uninterrupted for at least half an hour. Close the door, turn down the lights, and get comfortable. As you settle in, and as your mind begins to wander, begin the following visualization exercise about your ideal future:

Imagine that you're waking up in the morning—what time is it, where are you waking up, and whom are you waking up with?

Get out of bed and prepare to go to work. What kind of clothes do you put on? For what kind of work would they be suitable?

Imagine that you're now headed to your office. How do you get there? By car? Bicycle? Do you walk there? Is your office far away, or is it just down the hall?

You're opening the door to your office and walking in. Where is your office? What does it look like? How is it outfitted?

Are there others there with you in your office, or are you by yourself?

What kinds of products does your company stock and sell, or what kinds of services does it offer?

What do your customers look like? What kind of companies do they work for? How do they purchase your products or services? What do they

---

many copies as she could make for $20. Sylvie next set aside two days to go door to door, business to business, dropping off her flyers and making contacts with potential clients. She spent the next day making a lot of phone calls. Soon (within only three days) Sylvie had her first offer of work—calling

do with your products or services after they buy them? How do your products or services make your customers feel?

What do you say to your customers when you call them? What do they say to you when they call you?

Imagine that it's time for lunch. Where do you go, and whom do you eat lunch with? What do you talk about?

You go back to work after lunch. What do you do during the rest of the day? Whom do you talk with, where do you go, and what do you say?

Your workday draws to a close. Imagine putting your work away and preparing your office for your departure. What did you accomplish? What remains to be done tomorrow? What time do you depart, and where do you go?

Imagine arriving at your home. How do you feel? Are you happy? Sad? Energized? Tired? What do you do, and with whom do you do it? Do you take work home with you, or do you leave it behind at the office?

It's time to go to bed. What time is it? Is it easy for you to fall asleep, or does something keep you up?

As you work through your ideal day, think about what kind of business it is that takes you to the kinds of places you go and has you do the kinds of things that you do. Is there one business in particular that speaks most loudly to you, that excites you, that makes you look forward to starting your day?

local businesses and conducting marketing surveys with the president of the company to see whether it was interested in buying its printer cartridges from someone else. For this, Sylvie was paid $2 per successful survey and her new company was officially open for business.

Chances are, the reason you're stumped as to what business to start is because you're asking the wrong questions. You're probably wondering what you "could" do, what you "should" do, or what would be "best" to do and seeing either no truly appealing options or so many options that it's quite confusing. To get out of this rut, ask yourself an entirely different question: What would you like to be doing? If you could support yourself doing anything you want, what would you do?

> Changes in the economy make it possible for people to carve out unique niches doing rewarding kinds of work that no one would have ever hired them to do in the past.

In the past, most people had to settle for something more "practical" rather than what they would really like to do. The result? A lot of unhappy business owners, running businesses that didn't capture their hearts or their energy. But in this day and age, the "ideal" is often the most practical. Changes in the economy make it possible for people to carve out unique niches doing rewarding kinds of work that no one would have ever hired them to do in the past.

Who would imagine, for example, that a part-time custom fishing rod business would have any chance of success? Ian Scott would, that's who. Ian's idea was to build and sell custom fishing rods and tackle, and then plow the profits from these sales into a large wholesale order of custom fishing rod components. Sure enough, his niche idea worked, and Wishbone Custom Rods was born. Says Ian about the importance of moving forward with your dreams, "Never give up. Do something. Sometimes, do it differently, but keep the goal in sight."

Don't limit your future to outdated ideas of what's possible. Find a match between the lifestyle you desire, your experience and background, what you enjoy doing, and what people will pay for. The best work for you is the work that sparks your passion, allows you to apply your skills and talents, is energizing, builds your self-confidence and self-esteem, and allows you to make enough money to make it all worth your while.

Here are some tips for identifying the kind of work that will be best for you:

- *What kind of work do you dream about?* We all have a picture within ourselves of the kind of work that we dream about doing. The truth is, with sufficient training, an active customer base, and a bit of persistence, you can turn your dream job into your reality. When Monica Hogg created her first Web page, she unlocked a passion that surprised even her. Says Monica, "I loved it so much I soon became a woman obsessed and was making Web pages for everything I could think of. It wasn't unusual for me to be on the computer from the time I woke up to the time I went to bed." Overcoming her own self-doubts, she leveraged this passion into a thriving business: MonicaWorks of Mayne Island, British Columbia. According to Monica, dreams *can* become reality: "It's become clear to me that this is what I'm meant to do. Sometimes in life, things fall neatly into place, and that is certainly the way it happened with MonicaWorks."

  Key Questions: Have you ever considered the kind of business you would select if you could follow your heart and not worry about being practical? If not, what kind of business do you dream about having—what kind of business would unleash your passion and energy? Can you discover some way to turn your dream into a business that others would pay for its products or services? Have you explored all possible avenues for turning your dream into reality? If not, how can you do just that?

- *Where do your talents lie?* We all have talents and skills in different areas—where do *your* talents lie? It generally makes far more sense to pursue a business that allows you to leverage and capitalize on your already existing talents and skills rather than learning a completely new set from scratch. Imagine, for example, that you're a talented musician, and you are particularly gifted at teaching your musical skills to others. It makes far more sense for you to start a business giving music lessons—something you're already well versed in—than it does for you to start a business welding motorcycle frames, something you know nothing about. Years ago, former "welfare mom" Laura Knott Twine found that she had a talent for textile design and weaving. After showing her hand-woven creations at a number of juried arts and crafts shows throughout southern New England—and garnering many awards—Laura decided to turn her hobby into a fast-growing and successful home-based business, Orchard House Weavers. Laura's inspiring success story was featured in *Family Circle* magazine, on *CBS News,* and in more than two hundred print and electronic media outlets.

    Key Questions: What kinds of talents and skills do you have? Are you artistic? Organized? Do you have a knack for working with animals? Are you a natural mechanic? Do your friends and colleagues seek you out because you have some special talent that is uncommon or particularly noteworthy? Do you have a great recipe for homemade barbecue sauce? Why not start a business that capitalizes on your strengths and allows you to hit the road to achieving your dreams running?

- *Are you committed to a particular cause?* Some people find that their compelling belief in a particular cause or life's mission is all the motivation they need to jump-start their businesses. Are you a true believer in something? Are you driven to make a contribution to your family, your community, or your world? Many successful entrepreneurs were inspired to start their businesses because of their personal missions in life, whether it is serving God, giving disadvantaged people the tools and training they need to pull themselves out of a life of poverty, teaching children to read, or any number of others. What is your mission? From the age of six, when she picked her first tomatoes as a field hand in the Midwest, Linda Torres-Winters knew that she wanted to do something to help her family and to be somebody. Not only that, but Linda was driven to honor her Hispanic heritage in whatever endeavor she would eventually pursue. What she didn't know was that tomatoes would be such an important part of her future. Years later—after going to college (the first in her family to do so), marrying, and having two children—Linda's mission to make something of her life and to honor her heritage led her to start a business selling a unique product: Linditas' Instant Salsa Mixes. Inspired by her mother's own cooking, the salsa mixes are packages of dried spices and vegetables that, when added to fresh or canned tomatoes, result in "homemade" salsa anytime, anyplace. Linda's mission resulted in a very successful business; today, her products are available in more than five hundred stores in eight different states.

Key Questions: Do you want more out of your business than just to make money? If you could change the world with your business or make a positive contribution to your community, what kind of business would help you achieve your goals? Are there injustices that you would like to right or tragedies that you would like to help others better survive or avoid altogether? How can you transform your desire to make a real difference in the world into action?

As you dive into finding out more about a particular kind of business that you're interested in, you may find that there's far more involved than you personally want to commit to or are comfortable with. If that's the case, you may want to talk with some people who are already successfully doing what you want to do to see whether they have learned any shortcuts that you can take advantage of. Alternatively, you may simply

> The better prepared you are to start your business, the better chance it will succeed.

Every Day Is Christmas

While Cathy Hale's business—Santa Claus Productions, in Culver City, California—is today a roaring success, things weren't always so certain in her life. Cathy started her business (which provides Christmas-themed set decoration services to Hollywood film production companies; her credits include Jim Carrey's film *How the Grinch Stole Christmas*, Arnold Schwarzenegger's film *Jingle All the Way*, and many television shows and commercials) in 1985. She had recently quit her high-pressure job as a commercial real estate broker and had no idea what she would do next. Talking with her accountant one day—who happened to own several Christmas tree lots—he suggested that Cathy consider getting into the Christmas business. But, while Cathy's accountant sparked her idea for a business—and helped advise her during start-up—she knew nothing about starting and operating her own business.

Not letting this potential barrier get in her way, Cathy started calling local banks to see whether they had already made their Christmas tree–buying plans yet. At least forty had not, and they happily bought trees from her, while many that had already bought trees promised to buy

decide to try something else. Whichever way you decide to go, don't feel pressured by the expectations of others. This is *your* life that we're talking about, and it's you who has to be happy with it!

Once you've got an idea of the kinds of businesses you would like to start—you may have a number in mind, or you may have already narrowed down your choices to just one—it's time to conduct some very thorough research. The better prepared you are to start your business, the better chance it will succeed. Just don't forget that at some point you've got to stop researching and start taking action!

---

them from her the following year. Cathy's business was taking off. After buying out a decorator who was going out of business, Cathy found herself with sixteen boxes of Christmas decorations. Says Cathy, "All of a sudden I had sixteen boxes of Christmas decorations, so I figured I better do something with them." And that's exactly what she did. She founded Santa Claus Productions and began decorating for a wide variety of clients.

Her early displays were focused primarily on hotel and corporation lobbies. Soon, however, television and film production companies found out about her services, and they began to monopolize her schedule. As the production work ramped up, Cathy started another company focused solely in that area: Almost Christmas Prop Shop. According to Cathy, starting her own business—this particular business—was truly a godsend: "I prayed to God to help me find a business that spreads joy and is recession-proof. But most of all, I love doing Christmas because it's something that makes people happy." And it's clear that not only are Cathy's clients happy with the business she has chosen, but so is she, and it has made all the difference in the world to her.

IS THERE AN E-BUSINESS IN YOUR FUTURE?

A report based on two surveys sponsored by the National Federation of Independent Business and the Center for Women's Business Research found that small businesses have the most to gain by reorganizing as e-businesses. The report includes the following key findings:

The Internet offers unparalleled new opportunities for small businesses: 57 percent of small firms use the Internet, and 61 percent of those have a Web site.

A Web site gives entrepreneurs access to markets at low cost: 67 percent gained new customers; 62 percent improved competitive position; 56 percent increased total sales; and 56 percent attracted new types of customers.

Web sites are cost-effective for small niche businesses: 65 percent of firms make a profit or cover their Web site costs.

The smallest firms with fewer than ten employees benefit the most from being online: 35 percent gain 10 to 99 percent of current sales directly or indirectly from their Web sites.

Question 2: Who Will Pay Me to Do What I Want to Do?

You may have a pretty good idea of what kind of business you want to start but still be not quite ready to take the next step along the path to independence. Why? Because, despite the fact that you're excited about the business you've chosen, you just can't seem to imagine who is going to want to buy what it is that you've decided to sell. The fact is, for just about every conceivable product and service that you might ever imagine selling,

A MARRIAGE OF LOVE AND SUCCESS

Soon after meeting for the first time, Russian immigrants Laila Rubstein and Eugene Yushin found that they shared a common interest in multimedia. Computer science major Laila and artist Eugene decided to team up in two ways: marrying and then starting up their own business, Artec International. The only problem was, although they knew quite a bit about multimedia, they knew nothing about starting and running a business, much less whether such a business would be profitable for them.

After bouncing around a number of different ideas and conducting no small amount of research, the couple resolved that designing and marketing animated, colorful, and customizable multimedia greeting cards on the Internet would be the best way to take advantage of their mutual interests and talents, while also creating financial independence for themselves. Eugene started designing, and Laila started programming. Soon, the couple launched their pioneering Web site to distribute their new digital products around the world via the Internet. The result was the first digital greeting card store on the Web—a site that became a great success for the couple. As a result of their greeting card business, Eugene and Laila soon discovered that there was a huge demand for multimedia work in the corporate market. To supplement their growing income, the couple accepted digital animation work for corporate clients.

While it has been a lot of work—Laila and Eugene worked many fourteen-hour days at the beginning—it has all been worth it, both financially and in terms of the freedom they have to pursue their own dreams. Says Laila, "The best part of the business is that it's fun." And not only has it been fun for Laila and Eugene, it has been profitable.

there is a customer somewhere willing to buy it. And he or she will, so long as the price is reasonable, the quality is good, and your customer finds out about you and your new business.

Every business needs customers. Without customers, you don't really have a business, and, as far as the Internal Revenue Service is concerned, if you don't have customers, your "business" is in danger of being considered a hobby, and any tax deductions you've taken on your business will be disallowed—not a good thing.

Remember: You may have found what in your eyes is the greatest business in the world, but if people don't know that it exists, you'll soon find your dream slipping away from you. To find your way around this obstacle, therefore, you need to dedicate some serious time identifying your customers *before* you start your business, and then seriously marketing them as soon as your new enterprise is open for business.

> You may have found what in your eyes is the greatest business in the world, but if people don't know that it exists, you'll soon find your dream slipping away from you.

When Mark McGregor of Hamilton, Ontario, decided to start his own public speaking business, he couldn't imagine exactly who would want to pay for his services. Already the successful owner of a financial consulting business, creating a business based on speaking in front of paying groups was something altogether different, and unfamiliar, to him. Rather than allow this obstacle to stop him, however, Mark committed to meeting as many potential prospects as possible by doing lots of networking in his community. He joined a variety of speaker's organizations, including Toastmasters International and the Hamilton chapter of the Canadian Association of

Professional Speakers. He also created a promotional Web site (www.speakingofhearts.com), conducted a number of promotional mailings to attract the attention of prospective customers, and volunteered for a variety of organizations. As Mark says, "You've got to circulate before you can percolate!"

Here are some tips for preparing yourself to find the customers you'll need to get your business off the ground and to keep it growing in the future:

- *Create a profile of your ideal customer.* Marketing is all about determining the demographics—the age, gender, income level, geographic location, and so forth—of your intended customers and directing your resources to get your message to the people most likely to buy your products or services. What do your ideal customers look like— male or female, young or old—how old are they, and what kind of income do they make? How do they receive their advertising messages—through radio or television, on a grocery store bulletin board, or in a local newspaper or national magazine? Certain people will be more apt to buy your products or services than others; understand who these people are, and get to know them and their preferences in great detail.
- *Determine the features and benefits of your products or services.* Every business owner naturally believes that his or her products or services are the very best available. Are they? What are the exact features and benefits of your products and services? Who will these features and benefits attract, and why? Are there any features and benefits that your customers are indifferent to (and that you could cut, saving money in the process)?
- *List five reasons why your customers would rather buy from you instead of your competitors.* What is it about

your products or services that make them better or more attractive to purchase than those offered by your potential competitors? Make a list of five reasons why your customers will want to buy your products or services instead of your competition's, and focus on these reasons as you identify your potential customer base.

- *Decide where you will sell your product.* Where are you going to sell your product or service? Will you sell it on the Internet? Through word of mouth? By placing an advertisement in the Yellow Pages? Through craft fairs or farmer's markets? Where you sell your product will be mostly driven by where you will find your ideal customers and the best ways to transmit your marketing messages to them.

- *Research how much your potential competitors currently charge for their products and services.* Do you have any idea how much your competitors charge for their products and services? If not, you should. While your projected cost and profit will determine the way you set your own prices, so will your competition. Call to request price lists, or check your competitors' Web sites for pricing information.

- *Determine how much you will charge for your products and services.* One of the most important decisions you will make—not only for the ultimate profitability (and long-term viability) of your business but also for marketing purposes—is the prices that you set for your products and services. The price you charge for your products and services will have an enormous impact on whether your ideal customers will decide to buy them, and it will therefore have a dramatic impact on the long-term prospects of your business. The good news is that if you set the wrong price to start, you can always change it—although you had best change it quickly, before your potential customers decide to look elsewhere for their needs!

- *Estimate your total annual sales.* Based on what you know about your prospective customers—and about the prices that you plan to charge for your products and services— what kind of numbers do you expect to achieve for your business's annual sales? Will this number be enough to make the business worth your while? If not, what can you do to increase it? Do you need to find more customers? Raise your prices? Improve your distribution? Get into an entirely different business?

- *What is the growth potential of your business, and in what areas will it be?* If your business takes off and grows, where will this growth come from? Will you sell more products or services to your "ideal" customers (and, if so, how will they get your message?), or will you need to reach out to other prospects beyond those who will be most interested in what you've got to sell? Don't wait for your future customers to find you; figure out who they are going to be in advance and factor them into your thinking.

   Key Question: Finding that first customer is often a stumbling block for many new business owners. To find your way around this barrier, ask yourself, Who do I know who will buy my product or service right now? A friend? A relative? A neighbor? Someone from work? If the answer is not obvious to you, how can you get to know people who might buy what you have to sell? Consider the story of Mark McGregor, who networked with prospective customers by joining Toastmasters International and the Canadian Association of Professional Speakers. In a very short time after joining these organizations, he was introduced to far more people than he could ever have hoped to meet any other way.

Question 3: How Can I Start with What I've Got?

Now comes the moment of truth. You have a pretty good idea about what kind of business you are going to start, and you know who will pay you to do what you want to do. But you also know that there's more you could learn, and now you know how you could get it. That's your reality. That's your situation. Now you get to figure out how to proceed with whatever you can create.

If you know enough to get started, then you're ready to go. If not, go back over the things you should know and your resources for learning more. Are you sure you don't already know enough to get started? Are you using indecision about what business to start as an excuse for not going forward?

Maybe the simple fact is that you can't start as big as you'd like or as soon as you'd like. Maybe you'll have to keep your day job and start out small-time on the side (not a bad idea, as far as we're concerned). Maybe you'll have to work part-time while you get things going. Maybe you'll need more time to get just a bit more information before you announce the opening of your new business.

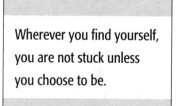

Wherever you find yourself, you are not stuck unless you choose to be.

Wherever you find yourself, you are not stuck unless you choose to be. Now you simply have to do whatever it is you need to do next, and then you will have gotten past the decision obstacle that's been hanging you up.

So, at this point, ask yourself:

What can I do now?

Not what do you *wish* you could do. Or what you *hope* to do. But what you actually *can* do now. Then do it. And keep

BUSINESS BIDDING

The Internet has brought with it all kinds of come-ons for home-business and self-employment "opportunities" that are in reality thinly veiled scams and rip-offs. The good news is that the Internet has also brought with it some very real business opportunities—the kind that can put you squarely on the path to achieving your dreams of independence. One such opportunity is online auction site eBay (www.ebay.com).

Before starting her own home-based business, Sandy Kleppinger of Leesburg, Virginia, had more than a few obstacles to overcome. As a stay-at-home mom homeschooling her twelve-year-old son in a small, rural town outside of Washington, D.C., Sandy had no business experience, no start-up capital, and no network of colleagues to rely on. All Sandy had was a burning desire to succeed and, as it turns out, that was exactly what she needed to succeed.

Today, Sandy's Finds brings in more than $100,000 a year. The spark for Sandy's company was ignited when she purchased one hundred boxes of closed-out software from a remainder bin at a local CompUSA store for less than one dollar each, then turned around and sold every box she had on eBay for an average of $10 each. By using eBay to sell her products, Sandy can easily work out of her home; she is able to reach an international audience of prospective customers; and she can spend more time with her family (her son Kory helps retrieve stock and package orders for shipping) and make a significant contribution to the family's finances all at the same time. Not bad for someone who didn't know anything about business before she got started.

moving ahead based on what you discover. Refuse to let uncertainty about what kind of business to start become a lifelong obstacle. Millions of people have gotten past this obstacle by doing whatever it is they can do right now. And so can you! Remember the words of Theodore Roosevelt: "Do what you can, with what you have, right where you are." And just keep asking . . .

What can *I do now?*

Our Bias

While the three questions presented in this chapter should get you on the right track to making your dreams of being your own boss a reality, we understand that some obstacles can be particularly tricky to deal with. Here are some that don't depend on what you know, along with our advice on what to do about them.

- *No one you talk to understands what you want to do.* So, what do you do when you've got the greatest ideas since ketchup in a bottle, but no one understands what you want to do, or, even worse, they think that whatever you want to do makes no sense at all? If you really believe in yourself—and in your idea—then you shouldn't let anyone turn you away from your dream. This doesn't mean that you should totally ignore what others say—you should always be open to other perspectives and opinions—but the truth is, the road to success is well paved with stories of highly successful entrepreneurs who were told that their ideas wouldn't work, or that they made no sense, or that no one would want to buy whatever it was they wanted to sell.

Believe in your ideas, and believe in yourself. Each one of us is capable of achieving the impossible if we are willing to set our minds to it.

- *You know what you want to do but lack skills or credible experience.* This may seem like an incredibly difficult obstacle to overcome, but it really doesn't have to be. A lack of experience, training, education, or other seeming prerequisites for starting a business are not barriers for the successful entrepreneurs that you read about in newspaper and magazine articles. Instead of thinking of all the reasons she couldn't start her own business, Sylvie Charrier made a list of all the things she *could* do. Once she did that, starting a business became easy for her. Instead of thinking of all the reasons why they can't start their own business, successful entrepreneurs think of all the reasons why they can—and they step their way around one big barrier in their path to independence.

  Some kinds of businesses require experience; others don't. And even for businesses that require some amount of experience, chances are that you can learn enough to get by in fairly short order, if you put your mind to it. Don't let a lack of experience get in your way or slow you down. Dive in—the water's fine!

- *You haven't put in enough time finding the answers.* Starting your own business and being your own boss is a lot of work. And if you do it the right way, researching the answers to your questions and learning first steps for starting your own business will be a lot of work, too. If you can't find the answers to your questions, chances are, you haven't put enough time into finding them. The answer? Go back to question 2 and do more research. Remember Michael Reagan, who set aside six months to research a variety of different business options? He eventually created a list of 103 different characteristics that were important to him in the business he would select. This list made it much easier for him finally to decide on the right business to start.

We have suggested a number of different approaches to finding the answers to your questions have you tried them all? Did you give certain ones short shrift? Whatever the case, you'll need to figure out what the answers are for yourself; we can't give them to you. So, before you allow this obstacle to stop your progress, get out there and do some more research!

From the issues and information in this chapter, identify three things you want or need to do to start your business. Write them down in the Personal Action Plan in Appendix A: Take-Off Section, beginning on page 294.

CHAPTER THREE

I Know What I Need to Do, but I Just Can't Get Myself Going!

There is so much to do, and it seems like I need to do everything all at once. How do I decide what to do when?

I can't afford employees, and I'm not a detail person. How do I motivate myself to deal with all these start-up details?

My schedule is already cram-packed. How am I supposed to find the time and energy to do all this?

How do I make room for family and job responsibilities and still work on my business?

But what if I fail?

You've decided on a business that will fulfill your dreams, and you know it's time to get started. You need to get your office set up in your home or elsewhere, get business cards, arrange for phone service, open a bank account, buy or lease a computer, sign up for an Internet connection, establish a system for tracking your income and expenses, develop your marketing materials, and so forth. But you haven't gotten around to doing these things.

For some reason, you're not making these start-up activities a priority in your life. Why? What's going on? When you just can't seem to get started, we find it's usually for one or more of four reasons we call the Balk Blocks:

- Decision-Making Deadlock: I'm Not Sure I'm Doing It Right
- Flabby Self-Management Muscle: I Have Trouble Getting Myself to Do Stuff I'd Rather Avoid
- Overbooked with No Juice: I Can't Find the Time or Energy
- Flight from Fright: The Possibility I Might Fail Scares Me

If any of these reasons sound familiar, it's not surprising. Most of us have little or no preparation to be our own boss. On a salaried job, many of the basic decisions of your day are already decided by the demands of your job description. Your supervisor is either looking over your shoulder or reviewing your work, and you have a staff of other people to handle the details of running the other aspects of the office.

Also, few people can devote their full attention to starting their business. Usually we've got to fit it in with a myriad of other responsibilities, obligations, and priorities. So, it's difficult to find the time and energy to make it all fit, especially if friends and family are pulling you in other directions. So, when push comes to shove, it's easy for our business plans to end up on the proverbial back burner—one of those things we'll get around to . . . someday. Then, of course, when you wander into the shadowy unknowns of self-employment, the specter of failure may be lurking in the background of your mind.

But these Balk Blocks don't have to put your plans on hold. You can step your way around them right now by asking the following questions:

Is one of these Balk Blocks stalling me?

What's going on that I'm balking?

How do I get moving again?

The good news is that once you get your business under way, it will begin to develop a momentum of its own, but only after you get it going. So, let's go through each of the Balk Blocks in detail so you can discover whether one or more is hanging you up and what you can do to get moving again.

Decision-Making Deadlock: I'm Not Sure I'm Doing It Right

Decisions, decisions, making up one's mind—is there anything harder than trying to decide? Starting up a business is filled with a zillion choices big and small, from whether to incorporate to which paper clips to buy. And they're all competing for your attention. You can't do everything at once, and, if you try, you usually end up getting nothing done at all. And with the wealth of choices we have today about everything from which brands of equipment to which insurance plans to sign up for, it's easy to get trapped in analysis paralysis, indecision, and inaction.

Is This You?
Do you chronically catch yourself saying any of the following signs of Decision-Making Deadlock?

❑ What if I make the wrong decision?

❑ I'm just not sure which choice is the best one.

❏ I just need a little more information or a little more time to think this over.

❏ What if this won't serve my customers?

❏ I've got to do this perfectly.

❏ I'd better play it safe.

❏ There's a better way to do this just around the corner.

WHAT'S GOING ON?

One of the reasons people want to go out on their own is so they can make their own decisions. But we don't usually give much thought to how we make decisions. We just make them . . . or not. So, if any of the above refrains has become your mantra, it's time to think about your approach to decision making and specifically which decisions you're avoiding or obsessing over.

To find out what's going on, make a list of the decisions hanging over your head, and write at least one sentence describing why you're avoiding or struggling with them. For example, are you being indecisive about any of these points?

What name to call your business

When you should leave your current job to start your business

To whom you're going to target your products

Whether to start your business out of your home or to rent office space

Whom you'll approach for capital to help fund your start-up

Furniture for your office

What equipment and other supplies you'll need to get your business off the ground

Getting the licenses and permits you need

Which Web site designer or hosting service to choose

WHAT YOU CAN DO

Decision making isn't a problem when you know what to do. But becoming self-employed presents many situations when you won't know what to do. That's when we balk at making decisions, but here are some ideas about what you can do.

Ask for Help

Even though you're on your own, you don't have to make your decisions alone. You can turn to experts and professional advisers (a lawyer, accountant, computer consultant, etc.) for help with some decisions. And you can talk through decisions with trusted peers and colleagues. Of course, even with good advice, ultimately you will be the one who must decide.

Give Yourself Permission Not to Know

In our culture, we're always supposed to know what to do, and if we don't, we assume we're deficient in some way. But we don't always know what to do, especially when it comes to running a business for the first time. Much of what you do in starting a successful business is an experiment from which you learn what works and what doesn't. So if you don't know, don't panic; you don't have to know. The first step to discovering anything is admitting that you don't know but want to.

Assume There's a Good Decision

Decision making goes more smoothly when you start from the premise that there's a decision awaiting you. At this moment, you may not know what to do, but assume you will be able to decide once you have the information you need. There's a world of information available on virtually everything imaginable. So, look for the info you need on the Internet with a search engine like Google. Or if you can't find what you need, an information researcher can find the answers to the even most arcane problems, often for only a few hundred dollars.

Ask the Right Questions

Good decision making starts with asking yourself good questions like these:

1. How do you want this to come out?
2. What's most important to you about this?
3. How will you know whether you've found the best answer?
4. What did you do in the past when you handled something like this successfully?
5. What's an example of one possible decision you might make?
6. How would that work out?
7. How do you know that?
8. What stops you from deciding this?
9. What would happen if you did (or didn't) make this decision?

Let Your Gut Guide You

Sometimes you're so attached to having something work out as you want it to that you'll make a decision even though the little voice in your head or the twinge in your stomach is whispering, "This isn't the right decision." At other times that little voice is saying, "Yeah! This is it! Go for it!" but your mind is hung up on a bunch of insignificant details. You can probably remember countless times in your life when you wish you had heeded that little voice.

To move ahead with confidence, you need to trust your gut. Listen to that inner sense of knowing that we call the inner compass. Even though you may make mistakes from time to time, at least they won't be mistakes you knew better than to make in the first place. As creativity consultant Roger von Oech reminds us, "Errors are stepping-stones to new ideas." Over time, you'll be able to use this inner compass wisdom as an "emotional check" to know when a decision is, or isn't, right for you.

Focus Your Attention on Results

When you're stuck in a quandary about how to proceed, instead of focusing on the problem, focus on your desired outcome. When you get lost in the complexities of what you don't know about what might happen, you lose touch with what you want, and you can get trapped in the details of the quandary itself.

If you saw a car speeding toward a friend, you wouldn't be of much help if you jumped in front of the car with your friend, would you? So, don't run headlong into the oncoming complexities of the decisions you need to make. Focus instead on what you want to accomplish with the decision you're making, and you'll have a better view of what needs to be done.

Wrestle and Let Go

After you've grappled for a while with a decision that's hanging you up, set it aside. Just let it go. Take care of other things you need to do. Or take a break. Meanwhile, your subconscious mind will be working on the decision. Often just the decisions you've been looking for will come to you spontaneously in the midst of doing something else.

Talk It Over

Sometimes when you obsess over a decision, you get nowhere, but when talking through the decision with someone else, you suddenly find that the best decision seems obvious. The person you're talking with may offer a new perspective or see a nuance you've overlooked because you're so close to the situation.

To talk out a decision, you don't to need to talk with an expert on the subject. In talking something through, you're not seeking advice. The value of talking things out lies in the opportunity it provides for you to organize your thoughts and to articulate and clarify them so someone else can understand the issues you're seeking to address. Your conversation is like holding up a mirror to your thought processes. From this vantage point, you can gain a better picture of the decisions you want to make.

Make a Jiffy Decision

When the decisions you have to make aren't momentous—like which paper clips to buy, which brand of paper to get (there are a million little decisions like this to make)—quickly gather the information at hand, process it, and make your decision on the spot. You can live with these decisions, even if they're not the best, so don't fret over them.

When All Else Fails, Pick One

When you're stuck in a decision you need to make to get started, it's usually better do to something than nothing. So if all else fails to get you going, pick something, do it, and see what you can learn about what you need to decide next time. Try these tips to make your pick:

Toss a coin.

Pretend you know what to do. Imagine you're a wizard, shaman, or clairvoyant. What would you decide?

Choose what seems like an impractical or illogical decision. Having made that choice may lead you immediately to a better, more logical and practical one.

Turn the decision into a story or a movie. What happens? How would the characters do it?

When you find the right answer, look for a second one. It may be better than the first.

Imagine doing what needs to be done as if you were moving backward from your desired outcome. How did you get there? This perspective may give you insight into how to move forward.

Consider how someone in another profession or field would approach this. What would an architect do in this situation? An actress? A farmer?

Pose the questions you're asking differently. What if the problem isn't what you think it is? As Emerson said, "Every wall is a door."

Ask what you think your mentor would decide in this situation.

Make an arbitrary choice.

In other words, try *something*. Test one particular choice in a small way first if possible and assess your results. If it wasn't the best decision, the results may suggest a better one.

Claim Your Rights

Good decision makers know they have the right to make their own decisions even if they're not always the correct ones. As one person told us, "On the job, my decisions go through so many layers of approval that I never get to find out what would happen if I followed my own judgment."

In his book *Life Choices*, Gordon P. Miller presents "A Decider's Bill of Rights." As you read through these rights, think how they might apply to the decisions you're balking at making.

- You have the right to decide something for yourself even if no one else thinks you should decide that way.
- You have the right to express your feelings to others in the context of explaining your choices.
- You have the right to say no without feeling guilty.
- You have the right to decide how you use your resources, including your time.
- You have the right to rely on your emotions to help you make good decisions.
- You have the right to share your opinion with the expectation that others will listen.
- You have the right to admit you made a poor decision, to do something about it, and to continue to make more decisions.
- You have the right to ask others to consider you when they make a choice.

According to Rob Steir, founder and CEO of MBAGlobal Net.com in New York City, to be successful in your own business, at some point you've got to decide either to start a business or not to—you can't have it both ways. Says Rob, "My dad used to say, 'Not to decide is to decide.' This trying stuff doesn't make any sense. Either you either start a business or you don't start a business. You can't be wishy-washy. I found myself saying the word *trying* all the time—trying to do this, trying to do that. If you're halfway in a company and you're hedging your bets because you have a full-time salary and you're trying to start a business on the side, forget it—it won't work. You have to change your words.

"When I describe what I want to do, I don't say *try* anymore. I have become much more positive. Words impact how you think about the opportunity. It may make a difference in how other people perceive you, too, and how you perceive yourself.

"You have to have to have a vision for the business that you want to start. You have to believe it's not as risky as it might be because you're involved and you really believe you can do it. And you've got to say to yourself that you're going to do it; you're not going to just try.

"It was a struggle for me for a period of time, but seeing other people doing it, and realizing that they didn't have anything more special than I did, gave me the confidence I needed. I've always had a pretty good confidence level, so I knew it wasn't really risky for me to do this. It was more, Who would I rather have do this—me or someone else? How risky really is it? Most people look at risk and think, 'Oh, my gosh, you're starting a business—how can you do that?' But if you believe in yourself, it's not really risky.

"I made up my mind. I took the basic steps you've got to take: You incorporate; you put business cards together; you start acting the part and not always hesitating to do things. You play the role—or be the role—not just think you want to do it. I had that language of 'trying' for a long time—and I can preach all the time about this stuff—but it ain't easy. You have to have a dream and a vision. If you're just doing it to make money, it's not the right reason. I wanted to build a legacy, a business that's going to last a long time. If I'm going to sink, I'm going to sink on my own efforts. But if I win and become extremely successful, then I did it myself."

Flabby Self-Management Muscle: I Have Trouble Getting Myself to Do Stuff I'd Rather Avoid

We're often asked what's the one thing it takes to become your own boss, and invariably we say, "A healthy self-management muscle." You know the muscle we mean. It's the one that's located between the brain and the bottom. There's probably no greater power than the power to follow through on what you say you want to do.

> Nine out of ten Americans make New Year's resolutions, but studies show that of that group, almost 80 percent fail to follow through.

We make a lot of promises to ourselves. We set goals, make New Year's resolutions, swear we'll do something (or never do something again), only to let ourselves down. *USA Today* claims that nine out of ten Americans make New Year's resolutions, but studies by Alan Marlatt from the University of Washington in Seattle show that of that group, almost 80 percent fail to follow through.

Whether it's being able to hit a golf ball just where you want it to go, deliver a project on time within budget, or get yourself to eat more healthfully, being able to count on yourself to deliver on what you want to accomplish is truly a gift. And, if you want to become your own boss, it's not an option; it's essential.

Is This You?
When it comes to doing what you need to do to get your business started, do you:

- ❏ Keep putting off things you swear you'll do?

- ❏ Excuse yourself by saying, "I'll get to it later"?

- ❏ Never get around to important items on your to-do list?

- ❏ Leave projects incomplete?

- ❏ Tell yourself, "This is too hard," "This is too boring," "This is too . . . [whatever]"?

WHAT'S HAPPENING?

As your own boss, you need to be your own coach, mentor, and manager. Just like the professional athlete or performer, your success or failure will depend on how good a coach, mentor, and manager you are. You're the one who will have to inspire, motivate, energize, catalyze, cajole, outfox, outmaneuver, outwait, and outpsych yourself to do your best precisely when you need to, even under pressure.

This means you've got to know yourself very well, so well that you know what will get you going, keep you going, and make sure you follow through on what needs to be done, even when you'd rather not do it and even when you feel like giving up.

We all have the capacity to become a good coach, mentor, and manager for ourselves, but this ability is like a muscle. If you don't use it, it grows flabby. Truth is, most of us get pretty lazy. We're so overmanaged by the structure of our lives that we rarely think of ourselves as the boss. We look for opportunities to slack off, see what we can

> Just like the professional athlete or performer, your success or failure will depend on how good a coach, mentor, and manager you are.

get away with, and try to do as little as possible whenever we can. It's part of how we cope with a 24/7 world when we're not the boss.

Well, you're on your own, you can slack off whenever you want to. You can get away with everything and try to get by with as little as possible. Self-employment is the hooky player's haven. There's no one there but yourself to keep you on track. No bad performance reviews. No peer pressure. You can get away with anything. You just won't achieve your goals, and you'll be back to pounding the pavement in search of a paycheck.

So, if you're having trouble motivating yourself to do the nitty-gritty stuff you need to do to get started, chances are your self-management muscle is pretty flabby.

Just what kind of boss are you to yourself? Usually we don't give much thought to this. We just fall into bossing ourselves the way our parents, teachers, or prior bosses did. So, how were your authority role models? Were they punitive? Unreasonable? Critical? Laissez-faire? Absent? Demanding? Or were they understanding? Encouraging? Defining? Firm? Clear? Helpful? And how did you relate to them? Did you respect them? Look up to them? Appreciate them? Or did you resent them? Curse or laugh at them? Call them names behind their backs? Did you circumvent them whenever you could or try your best to live up to their expectations?

You're probably treating yourself pretty much the way they treated you and responding pretty much the way you responded to them. Whatever problems you have with authorities, when you are your own boss, you get to have them with yourself because now you are the authority.

What You Can Do

To develop your self-management muscle and get yourself motivated to do what needs to be done, think of yourself as your own protégé—your most important project. Your task is to get to know yourself so well that you can be a good manager to yourself even with all your bumps and warts. So, what motivates you? What de-motivates you? What can you say to yourself to get yourself going? What can you say to yourself that will turn you off or send you into a funk?

Start noticing what you respond positively to and what you don't. Pay attention to your preferences and needs, and respect them. Appreciate your natural abilities, and play to them. Recognize your limitations, and learn to take them into account, instead of fighting yourself to try to be who and what you're not.

Play to Your Motivators

Some people are motivated by one thing, while others are motivated by something else altogether. When visitors to Entrepreneur.com were asked, "What motivates you the most to start a business?" the answers were as follows:

To do what I love: 57 percent

To make money and then sell the business: 24 percent

To be my own boss: 19 percent

What motivates you? Here are some particularly strong motivators for many people thinking about starting their own business:

To have financial security

To compete and to win

To be independent

To be able to provide for loved ones

To complete a difficult challenge

To have autonomy

To do meaningful work

To have others recognize one's success

To control others

To attain financial success

To be treated fairly

To be in charge

To do what one loves

To be liked by others

Whenever you get bogged down in not wanting to do what you need to do to achieve your plans, remind yourself of what motivates you, and use the energy of that to charge you up and get you going. When you're procrastinating, ask yourself, "Do you still want to be your own boss? Do you still want to be independent?" Connect with the passion that drew you to go out on your own in the first place.

Find a Balance

Motivation is a fragile thing. It has to be nurtured, fed, and acted on in the right measure. If not, it fades or, worse, deteriorates into negative feelings and self-defeating attitudes. If you drive yourself relentlessly and treat yourself with disrespect, you will rebel or burn out, often without even realizing what you're doing to yourself. On the other hand, if you don't use your self-management muscle, you may well disappoint yourself.

So, make a list of the traits you would use to describe a good boss, and treat yourself accordingly. Here are some important Motivation Do's and Don'ts when you're the boss:

• Do set goals for yourself, and make plans for achieving them. Success does not happen by accident; success happens by intention.

• Do take small steps toward your goals. There's no need to take on the world all at once—go at your own pace and take your time. By biting off a little at a time, you're less likely to become overwhelmed by your goals and far more likely to attain them.

• Do concentrate on your strengths and not your weaknesses. We are all better at some things than we are at others. Don't waste your time trying to become something you're not—take advantage of the things you're best at.

• Do make commitments. Make firm commitments to achieving your goals, but stay motivated by breaking them into chunks you can achieve.

• Do reward yourself whenever you achieve a key goal. Give yourself a pat on the back, take the afternoon off, see a movie, go shopping—whatever makes you feel good.

• Don't compare your accomplishments (or lack thereof) to the accomplishments of others. You are unique, and your path to success is your own.

• Don't focus on what you can't do; focus on what you can do.

• Don't obsess about your past failures. Look to the future, and keep moving forward, toward your goals.

• Don't throw out your values and beliefs to achieve your goals. Be true to what you value and believe, and you will be more highly motivated to achieve your goals.

• Don't depend on others to achieve your goals. You can certainly enlist support from others, but no one cares as much about your business as you do, and you can't count on others to place your priorities ahead of their own.

In a Pinch, Use This Quick-Start Tip

If you're having trouble getting down to business, psychologist Stanley Coren of the University of British Columbia suggests using this formula:

Most Important + Easiest + Quickest = Best Place to Start

Make a list of what you want to accomplish during a particular work period. Identify which steps are the most important and which you can do the most quickly and easily. Then start with the most important steps you can do most quickly and easily.

Until about a year ago, Alyssa Chen had no reason to consider working for herself. Why should she? She had a great job with Be Free, an online marketing service in Marlborough, Massachusetts, and her future looked very bright indeed. At least until the company conducted a huge round of layoffs, removing Alyssa's boss and her boss's boss.

"I was fortunate in that they never laid me off," Alyssa says, "but the layoffs affected me. I felt like, 'Oh, my God, what am I doing with my career?' It got me thinking about what it is I've always wanted to do." When Alyssa found a business card for the Paperie, a seller of invitations and paper products in San Diego, California, she had an idea she might not otherwise have had. "I sent an e-mail to the managing partners of the store," she recalls, "saying 'Hey, you know, I'm thirty-odd years old, and I have an MBA and a passion for paper products. I would love to talk to you about doing some type of a partnership out here on the East Coast.'" The owners of the company agreed, and Alyssa will open her own Paperie store in Boston within the next six months.

The timing was perfect for Alyssa. She was going through a divorce, and that summer was a turning point. "We sold our house. My cost of living is down, and I don't have a mortgage. So, I can rely on funds from the sale of the house to get me through the first year or year and a half."

Overbooked with No Juice: I Can't Find the Time or Energy

Does it seem like there's always something in your life that comes between you and the exciting prospect of starting the new business you've been dreaming about so you can finally become your own boss?

Is This You?

- ❏ Too busy with the kids, family activities, or volunteer commitments?

- ❏ Consumed with the demands of your salaried job, bringing work home or spending extra hours at the office?

- ❏ Just plain exhausted to the point that when you get home from work, all you want to do is relax and watch television?

- ❏ Distracted from working on your business by demands from family and friends to spend more time with them instead of on your business?

WHAT'S HAPPENING?

The simple answer to this simple question is this: Your business won't be a priority until you make it a priority. It won't happen until starting your business is important enough for

> The fact is, if something is important enough in your life—if you really want it badly enough—you will find the time to do it, and you will have the energy to do it.

you to make room for it in your life. The fact is, if something is important enough in your life— if you really want it badly enough—you will find the time to do it, and you will have the energy to do it. We all have priorities, and our top priorities get done. It's the priorities down the list that languish. Those are the ones that never seem to get done. If you want to get something done on your business, you've got to find a way to put it at the top of your list.

WHAT YOU CAN DO

Ask the Hard Questions

If time is passing and you're not finding room in your life to start your business, it's time to take another look at whether you really want to do this. It's okay if you don't. Maybe it's not what's most important to you right now after all. Review this key question: Why do you think you want to be your own boss?

To get away from a job you hate?

To do what you love?

To impress someone else?

Is starting your own business truly your goal, or do you just like to fantasize about leaving your current job or office politics behind for something new and exciting? Are you entertaining the thought to meet someone else's expectations?

If you really don't want to go out on your own *for whatever reason,* don't do it. Give yourself a break and get on with what you really want to do. Don't give yourself a moment's grief about changing your mind. Sometimes we have to get right up to the point of making a change before we realize it's not really what we want to do.

If you find that you still want to be your own boss, then it's time to ask the next hard question: Are you sure you've chosen the right business?

Do you get butterflies in your stomach every time you think about starting and operating the business you've chosen?

Does the thought of actually doing it make you nauseous?

Do you sigh a lot at the prospect of getting under way?

Does your heart sink a little when it's time to get down to business?

If any of these answers fits you, go back to chapter 2 and reconsider the business you've chosen for yourself. Again, sometimes we have to get into doing something before we realize it's not what we thought it would be.

Set Goals

When you're highly motivated and don't have many distractions or responsibilities other than to pursue your business plans, regular goal setting is less important because your goals are at the forefront of your mind, and there's not much that can keep you from pursuing them. But if you have many other pressing demands, priorities, and responsibilities, your business plans can easily slip off the calendar unless you consciously put daily, weekly, or monthly goals on your list of things to do.

Although anyone can start a business at any time with little or no forethought, the most successful (and longest-lasting) businesses didn't just happen by accident—they were the result of deliberate action. Their founders put no small amount of effort into planning their success and creating goals and milestones to keep them motivated and to help them measure their progress along the path to success.

So, when you set your goals, be sure to set SMART goals. SMART goals are described as follows:

> Although anyone can start a business at any time with little or no forethought, the most successful (and longest-lasting) businesses didn't just happen by accident—they were the result of deliberate action.

Specific. Be clear and unambiguous. Write down your goals. When you read them, you should be able to see quickly what you mean to do, and so should others who read them.

Measurable. Goals should be written so you can measure your progress toward meeting them—for example, not "Make progress" but "File my DBA."

Attainable. Be sure your goals are realistic, not fantasies that you could only attain through heroic effort. To be realistic, you may need to split large goals into smaller, "bite-size" ones that can be more readily accomplished—for example, not "Write a book" but "Create an outline for a book."

Relevant. Each goal should bring you closer to your desired destination, and nowhere else, so relate goals to specific outcomes.

Time bound. Your goals should have deadlines with a definite beginning and end of a fixed duration. "I will apply for an SBA loan no later than Friday" is much better than "I will apply for an SBA loan."

According to the Small Business Administration, 97 percent of the population does not set goals. Why? (1) Fears that prevent them from doing so and (2) the risk of not attaining them. Both these reasons stem from a pessimistic attitude about the outcome. "Optimism," says Michael Mercer, business psychologist and coauthor of *Spontaneous Optimism* (Castlegate Publishing), "is solely a habit. It's not genetic, and it's not something you breathe in the air. Optimistic entrepreneurs lay out clear goals for how they want their businesses to succeed, make realistic timetables, and spend 50 percent or more of their time focused on achieving those goals."

Larry Voss, cofounder of Paperchine, Inc., a manufacturer of paper-making equipment, parts, and services in Rockton, Illinois, says, "You can't finish what you don't start. I . . . believe that a step, followed by another step, will move you toward your personal goals. I remember one time helping a friend train for a triathlon during his last two weeks before the race and then being talked into participating myself. With only two weeks' training, I was ill prepared to be competitive, but I finished. During the event, it became one step followed by another until the conclusion, which proved to me that if you start and keep yourself moving, you can finish."

Key Questions: Are you setting daily, weekly, or monthly goals for starting your business? Are they specific enough to act on, and are they attainable? How can you divide the task of starting your business into a number of small goals so you can accomplish them by your target dates?

Get on a Plan

Setting goals is useless unless they get onto your schedule. But just putting goals on your to-do list is equally useless if you can't get to them. Moving them forward from day to day on your list but never crossing them off is just discouraging. So, we suggest starting your business on a reasonable timetable that enables you to proceed at a reasonable pace. Which of the following plans best suits your needs?

• *Fast Track—The Daily Plan.* Put yourself on the Fast Track if you can realistically do five activities a day toward starting your business and follow through on five others you initiated the day before. If so, set a goal to initiate five activities a day and follow through on five activities. Should you find yourself consistently slipping on this daily plan, try shifting to the Steady Track.

• *Steady Track—The Weekly Plan.* Put yourself on the Steady Track if it's more reasonable for you to set a goal to initiate five new activities a week toward starting your business and following through on five others you've initiated previously. If you find yourself consistently slipping on your weekly goals, shift to the Slow but Sure Track.

• *Slow but Sure Track—The Monthly Plan.* If it's unrealistic to think you can complete five goals a week and follow through on five others, get on the Slow but Sure Track. Set a goal to initiate five activities and follow through on five activities every month. If your life is filled with other commitments and responsibilities, you will probably make more progress on this monthly plan than you would by becoming discouraged from trying and failing to keep on a daily or weekly plan. The key to success lies not in the rate of your progress but in the fact that you make regular, consistent progress.

If you find the monthly plan is too demanding, you need to reevaluate whether becoming your own boss is really a priority for you right now. It's difficult for your business to develop any momentum if you can't initiate at least five goals and follow through on at least five goals a month. Momentum is vital because as your business develops a pattern of sustained forward movement, it takes on a life of its own, and progress becomes easier and easier as the momentum grows.

Set aside "sacrosanct" time to work on your business. If your goals have to make it into your day, week, or month on a catch-as-catch-can basis, they probably won't be achieved. So, commit to your plans by setting aside a specific time each day, week, or month when you will work on your business. Designate this time as sacrosanct, meaning that other events are scheduled around it and that you won't make exceptions. Inform everyone who needs to know that you won't be available during these times, and don't give yourself any wiggle room other than illness or dire emergencies.

> It's difficult for your business to develop any momentum if you can't initiate at least five goals and follow through on at least five goals a month.

It's important that you avoid choosing a time when you know you'll be tired, exhausted, interrupted, or competing with something else you'd really like to do. For most people, for example, right after you come home from work would not be a good time. Nor would a time during the weekend when you can predict family members will be begging you to do something with them, like going to the kids' Saturday morning soccer games.

Reward Your Progress

As you achieve weekly or monthly goals, be sure to reward yourself for the progress you're making! If you put off all the rewards and celebrations until the end, the journey becomes arduous, dreary, and dull. So, treat yourself along the way.

Hawaii-based online business owner Judith Kautz has a simple but effective system for rewarding her progress. She lines up a row of candy kisses along the side of her desk. As she completes a goal—for example, when she mails out a marketing piece—she rewards herself with a kiss. Periodically she adds other rewards to pique her interest; her current favorite is taking her phone off the hook for a little bit and turning on some relaxing music.

YOUR EMOTIONAL VOLUME KNOB

Scientists report that they have discovered a region of the brain that is suspected to magnify or mute bad moods. This region, located just a few inches behind the bridge of the nose, is termed the *ventromedial prefrontal cortex.* In their study, the scientists found that increased brain activity in this area was directly associated with bad moods. And, while other areas of the brain are associated with the creation of a variety of different emotions, it is thought that perhaps the ventrome-

---

MOOD MAGIC

To change your mood, try this: Find a bright light, then close your eyes and look into it. Sunlight is best, but a bright indoor light will do; just be sure that the light is something you're looking up at. Keep looking at the light for one to two minutes without opening your eyes. Then lower your head, open your eyes, and look over your right shoulder. Focus your gaze on whatever you see there for another minute. Then repeat this process, beginning with looking at the light, but this time look over your left shoulder. Notice the change in your mood.

dial prefrontal cortex acts as a sort of volume knob for these emotions, either turning them up or turning them down.

Flight from Fright: The Possibility I Might Fail Scares Me

Most people find the "no guarantees" world of starting your own business to be at least a little scary. Who wouldn't? But those who get started "feel the fear and do it anyway," as Susan Jeffers, author of a book by that name, says. For others, just doing it anyway is too uncertain a prospect to get past their concerns. After all, isn't it well known that most new businesses fail in the first year?

This urban myth has scared many people out of becoming their own boss, so let's get that roadblock out of the way once and for all. You've probably heard the oft-quoted statistic that most people who start a business don't get past their first year. It's been repeated over and over in the media, in how-to books, and from well-meaning friends hoping you'll think twice before trading your stable career for the murky unknown of starting your own business. With such dire odds, who wouldn't get just a little bit anxious about self-employment? It sounds like the deck is stacked against you before you even have a chance to get started?

But let's look at the facts, because facts dispel fears.

We understand that this dismal statistic actually came about by mistake some years ago when the then-director of the Small Business Administration misread a speech that was widely reported in the press. His text stated, "Most small businesses that fail, fail in the first year." Instead, he read, "Most small businesses fail in the first year." The fact is, this commonly cited statistic is not just misleading but is flat-out wrong. In truth, most businesses close for reasons other than failure. The Census Bureau has found that 57 percent of small businesses are successful at the time of closing.

Sensational statistics like those quoted in the wake of the dot-com closures of 2000 were sobering, but they, too, are another example of distorted information that leads to unnecessary fear and inaction. These closures were industry-specific and probably have nothing to do with what you want to do. Irrational fears engendered by sensationalized statistics are best countered by taking the time to get the facts about the success rates in your particular field or area of interest. Rather than succumbing to fears, find the facts and base your decisions and feelings about your prospects for success on your assessment of the market in your field, your own track record, and your specific situation.

> The Census Bureau has found that 57 percent of small businesses are successful at the time of closing.

Now, setting aside concerns about business survival statistics, let's address the rash of other fears that the prospect of going out on our own can trigger.

Is This You?

- ❑ Every time I get ready to write the check to borrow money to start my business, I freeze up.
- ❑ I keep saying to myself, "What if I don't make any money?"
- ❑ What if I lose everything?
- ❑ I know entrepreneurs are supposed to take risks, but me? I don't like risks.

❏ Just the thought that the day I leave my job is right around the corner makes me break out in a cold sweat.

WHAT'S HAPPENING?

Let's face it: The thought of leaving the relative security and familiarity of the job world—with its steady paycheck, benefits, and perks—can be threatening to anyone, and it's especially threatening if the economy is in one of its periodic down cycles.

A study of entrepreneurial activity in the United States conducted by Babson College and the Kauffman Center for Entrepreneurial Leadership found that interest by would-be entrepreneurs in starting new businesses waned in 2001, for example, when entrepreneurial activity in the United States dropped from 16.7 percent of adults in 2000 to only 11.7 percent in 2001—a drop of 30 percent. So, why such a big drop?

The lead researcher for the study, Babson College's Andrew Zacharakis, says, "Innovation and willingness to take risks often take a hiatus during times of [economic] instability, especially in the face of the technology backlash" that occurred with the Internet bust.

> Ironically, the greatest opportunities historically to succeed on your own occur when the economy is either on the wane or on the rise.

In other words, prevailing economic times have a profound effect on our confidence to head out on our own. Ironically, the greatest opportunities historically to succeed on your own occur when the economy is either on the wane or on the rise. So, the times during which people are the most afraid to go out on their own are actually the best times to do so.

SUCCESS AFTER FAILURE

Soon after Calvin Helin started his first company—a fishing business—it failed. For some people, failing at their first business effort might have prevented them from ever attempting to start up another business for fear of failing again. But Calvin refused to let fear rule his life. He went on to get a law degree and started two new enterprises after he graduated, the Calvin Helin Personal Law Corporation and Aboriginal Global Investment Management Ltd. Calvin's new businesses were so successful that he was named one of the *Financial Post*'s annual "Top 40 under 40" (the top forty Canadian businesspeople under forty years of age).

Says Calvin, "They say if you don't buy a ticket, you can't win the prize. I think I am a bigger risk taker now because I'm more prepared to fail. If you've failed once, well, that's your Ph.D. in business!"

The reasons are simple. During downturns or upturns, many businesses are tooling up and looking to expand without encumbering themselves with the cost of full-time employees, so they turn to the outside services of small businesses and self-employed individuals instead. At the same time, consumers either haven't given up hope yet or are eager from pent-up demand to buy again after tight times end.

Regardless of economic times, if your fears have put your efforts on hold, we have some tools to enable you to get past your concerns. If your fear of failure is rooted in a history of previous failures, we suggest you turn immediately to chapter 7. For everyone else whose fears are causing them to balk, let's consider what you might do to get past the fears that are stopping you.

What You Can Do

Understanding the biological role that fear plays in our lives can help you understand why it's popping into your life right now. Fear is a primal emotion that has evolved in humans (and in animals before us) over millions of years. Fear triggers what's called the *fight-or-flight response,* nature's way of preparing our bodies to deal with a life-threatening emergency. So, let's say you're walking along a path in the African savannah when, all of a sudden, a lion jumps onto the path only twenty yards in front of you. As soon as your eyes see that lion, a part of your brain called the *hypothalamus* sends an immediate message to your adrenal glands to start dumping adrenaline into your bloodstream. As the adrenaline begins to circulate, your heartbeat speeds up dramatically—doubling or even tripling—pushing blood into your muscles. Your digestion stops, your immune system shuts down, the capillaries under your skin are turned off, and your eyes dilate. You're instantly stronger and more alert. You are ready for action.

In short, your body is prepared to do one of two things: fight that lion or run away as fast as you can. In this sense, fear is a very helpful emotion to have when you find yourself in a life-threatening situation—it can literally save your life. But fear can also be triggered by things that are not life-threatening. If these fears prevent you from doing the things you want to do, they're counterproductive and are doing you more harm than good.

At this point you may be saying, "I'm not afraid of being my boss! That's not what this resistance is about." But before you close the door on this possibility, consider this: You may have lived with your fears for so long that either they're so buried that you don't notice them, or you've become so used to their being there that they've become an integral part of your worldview, and you think they are realities and not fears.

Aside from the physical effects we described, which you no longer notice, fear can park itself in the middle of your path to independence in other ways that can stop you dead in your tracks. It can:

make you unwilling to change;

immobilize you;

cause you to withdraw and hide;

make you feel insecure;

create confusion;

stifle your creativity and motivation;

shake your self-confidence

Fear can even lead you to change your beliefs about life—and not for the better—actually altering your attitudes about the risks you're willing to take and what paths you're willing to pursue in life. So, take a look at your beliefs about life that may have been changed or molded by fears you're denying or glossing over. For example, pay attention to any belief or thought that contributes to your thinking that you can't be your own boss. Do you ever say to yourself things like these?

Why bother? I'm not going to succeed anyway.

Who would want to buy anything from me?

I've always worried about things like this, and I always will.

If I leave my job, no one will ever want to hire me again.

Things never go my way.

If I can't help myself, how could anyone else help me?

I'm not the salesperson type.

I'll never make as much money as I do in this job.

I deserve to fail.

The key to dealing successfully with fear is to be honest with yourself about it so you can stop denying your fears and start creating positive beliefs and patterns of behavior to replace them. It's also important to put a name to just what it is you're afraid of. As long as your fear is a vague feeling, you can't do anything about it. But once you identify what's triggering your fight-or-flight response, you can check out the reality of the situation and do something about your concerns.

> The key to dealing successfully with fear is to be honest with yourself about it so you can stop denying your fears and start creating positive beliefs and patterns of behavior to replace them.

So, what's making your heart beat faster? What's raising your blood pressure? What's turning your hands cold and clammy? Some common fears—any of which can easily become barriers on your path to independence—include these:

Fear of punishment

Fear of rejection

Fear of making a mistake

Fear of being alone

Fear of failure

Fear of making a decision

Fear of asking for what you want

Fear of change

Fear of technology

Fear of financial instability

Fear of the unknown

Here's a four-step process for discovering, naming, and replacing any fears that are holding you back.

Step 1: Identify Your Fears

Find a quiet place where you can sit down and relax for at least fifteen or twenty minutes. After you've had a few minutes to clear your mind, imagine yourself finally stepping over the obstacles that are getting in the way of your path to independence—imagine yourself starting your own business. How do you feel? Are you fearful of the changes that you now have to deal with or of the people who you'll have to answer to?

Ask yourself the following questions, and write your answers in the space on the next page:

- What is holding me back?
- Am I afraid of what will happen if I do what I want to do? Why?
- What worries are keeping me awake late at night?
- What exactly is it that is stopping me from doing what I want to do?
- Are there people who don't approve of my plans or are trying to disrupt them? Who and why?

- What kinds of bad things might happen to me if I do what I want to do?

Write your answers here:

When you're finished with your list, rank your fears in order from most powerful and destructive to least.

Step 2: Understand the Impact of These Fears on Your Life

After you've had a chance to write down your fears, go back to the top of the list and look at each one of them in order. What thoughts go through your mind as you read them? What scripts do you repeat (i.e., "I've never been good enough to . . ."), what negative thoughts or feelings do they bring up (i.e., "Most businesses fail anyway"), and what self-defeating beliefs and attitudes do you find yourself dredging up from the depths of your subconscious (i.e., "I'll never be successful")?

Write these thoughts down here, next to each of the fears that triggered them in the list you created in step 1.

1.

2.

3.

4.

5.

6.

7.

8.

9.

10.

Now, read through your fears and the thoughts that accompany them, and think about how they impact your life. How have your fears kept you from pursuing your dreams? How have they influenced the decisions you've made in your life—good and bad—the people you've developed relationships with, the jobs you've taken, the activities you've pursued? How do they disable you and inhibit you from taking action? How have your fears negatively impacted your self-confidence and feelings of self-worth? How do your fears continue to impact your life—and the decisions you make—today?

You can now see beyond a shadow of a doubt the power that fear holds over you, and you should have a better understanding of the critical importance of your overcoming it.

Step 3: Create New, Positive Responses to Your Fears

At this point your goal is to confront, update, and replace the negative, self-defeating thoughts that underlie your fears with positive and constructive ones based on what you know you can do with confidence in the context of your actual, factual situation. This means evaluating your situation to determine what, if anything, you have to fear and then making constructive plans that counter your irrational beliefs with the truth.

Many of our fearful beliefs were laid down when we were helpless children or otherwise powerless. But you are not powerless now. You are capable and have many resources at your command. So, make a conscious effort to correct negative beliefs that aren't supported by your current reality.

For example, if you have the self-defeating belief that "I will never be successful," review the times in your life when you have been successful and the reasons you know you can be successful now. If realistic doubts remain about the prospects of your future business, set out to find evidence to shore up your case for success. Or alter your plans to address your realistic concerns. Then lay out your case in clear terms, so you can confidently replace your outdated fears that you'll never succeed with the positive affirmation: "I will be successful."

> As your own boss, you can always alter your course and your goals as needed along the way to assure that you will indeed be successful.

This statement is a fact because as your own boss, you can always alter your course and your goals as needed along the way to assure that you will indeed be successful.

Use this process to go through the list you created in step 2, turning each of your negative thoughts and beliefs into positive ones. List them here:

Step 4: Stop Your Fears in Their Tracks

You want to clear out all the old thought patterns that hold your fears in place, and you can only do that by bringing them to the surface where you can evaluate and update them.

Starting today, each time you find yourself facing a fear or repeating a negative thought or belief in your mind, STOP! Catch yourself and replace the fear or negative thought or belief with a positive one from your earlier list. Doing this may bring forth a rush of additional negative thoughts, feelings, or beliefs. This reaction is fine, even typical. You want to clear out all the old thought patterns that hold your fears in place, and you can only do that by bringing them to the surface where you can evaluate and update them.

If it seems overwhelming to take on all your fears at once, you may feel more comfortable selecting the most destructive fear or belief from your list and starting there. Then work your way down the list as you address each fear. In this way, slowly but surely, you will replace your fears and negative

---

PLAYING IT SAFE AT FIRST

Dan Dorotik, founder and president of Career Documents, a resume-writing service located in Lubbock, Texas, started his own business not because he had a dream of being his own boss but because he found himself suddenly out of work when he left his job as a teacher to move with his fiancée to a different city.

Like everyone else starting their own business, Dan was nervous about making the transition. But he countered his fears by working part-time jobs while he built his business. In this way, he assured himself of having a steady income.

Soon he saw that his clients were willing to pay him a good sum of money to do their resumes. His business is doing great. Dan says, "All you hear about in the media is the failure of the dot-coms and the failures of start-up ventures, so people think 'So many people have failed. How am I going to make it?' That's why I put up safeguards to cover for possible tough times. But, when I saw the money coming in, I realized that if you're really good at something—and if you're smart at the business and marketing side of it while maintaining the quality of the work—you can make a very good living for yourself."

thoughts with new ones that will support you in safely taking action to create a new life for yourself.

Mila Radulovic, founder of the New York City–based Internet content syndication firm Fashion Icon, Inc., inherited a handy tool for doing this from her father. "From the age of two," she explains, "I grew up hearing my Yugoslavian father's motto: '*Napred nasi*,' which means 'Never give up.' By simply not giving up, you can do anything." Since that time, Mila updated this motto to "I can do anything," and as a continual reminder, she strategically posts it around her home and office (e.g., on her notebooks, drawing board, fax machine, and computer screen). You might want to do the same with the new messages you want to keep in mind.

From the issues and information in this chapter, identify three things you want or need to do. Write them down in the Personal Action Plan in Appendix A: Take-Off Section, beginning on page 294.

CHAPTER FOUR

But I Don't Have the Money!

I don't have any money—how can I start a business?

How could I ever come up with that kind of money?

What would I live on while I get the business going?

What if I run out of money?

Money—that is, the lack of money—tops the list of worries that keep people tethered to the paycheck. And it's not surprising. Money, the SBA tells us, is the number one reason for business failure. It cites specifically "lack of capitalization," meaning that the business ran out of money before it could start making a profit.

Unfortunately, this oft-quoted fact causes many people who wish to go out on their own to get caught up in the mistaken belief that they'll have to raise some enormous sum of money or get approval for a big loan. Actually, few start-ups require much in the way of cash to get started. If you plan to hire one hundred people and purchase $1 million of inventory within the first thirty days from getting underway, then, yes, you'll need some major financial resources. But chances are that's not what you have in mind. If it is, it's not where you're going to need to start. Most people can get on their own for a very nominal sum of money—especially if you start from home, as seven out of ten new businesses do.

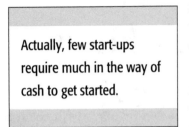

Actually, few start-ups require much in the way of cash to get started.

So, if lack of money is stopping you, here's what you can do right now. Don't assume you don't have enough money or that you can't get what you need. Step your way around this problem by addressing the following questions:

1. How much money do I *really* need?
2. How much do I *really* have?
3. How can I get more if there's a gap?
4. How can I start with what I've got?

Let's go through these questions in detail. By the time you're done with this chapter, you'll have a new perspective on how much money you've got and how much you need. Best of all, money will no longer be a barrier to your getting started, and you should be well on your way to moving along the path of making your dreams of independence reality.

Question 1: How Much Money Do I *Really* Need?

Do you know how much money you'll need to get started? Are you sure? Most people get struck with a double whammy of money fallacies:

- *The Overestimating Fallacy.* Most people who want to go out on their own overestimate how much money it will take to *start up their businesses*. Instead of just starting

COOKING UP A WINNING BUSINESS

A little more than twenty years ago a suburban housewife named Doris Christopher decided that she wanted to start her own business for the same reason that many people do: so that she could work flexible hours and spend more time with her young children. Doris had long known the value of having high-quality cooking tools and utensils in her kitchen, and her idea was to sell these same items to others through home demonstration parties. But Doris needed money to start her new business—The Pampered Chef—something in short supply for her and her family. The solution? Doris borrowed $3,000 from a life insurance policy to fund her start-up. With this money, she purchased a modest inventory of items to sell, as well as food to use in her in-home demonstrations (she sold $175 worth of kitchenware that first night). Today, The Pampered Chef has more than $700 million in annual sales and seventy thousand kitchen consultants who give more than nineteen thousand in-home demonstrations each week.

with what they have access to, they wait until they have some large amount they think they need to get going. The result? That time never comes. Opportunities pass. Their good ideas are snatched up by others. And they're still tethered to their paycheck.

- *The Underestimating Fallacy.* Most prospective business owners underestimate the amount of money they will need to *operate their businesses*—that is, to keep the business and themselves afloat and growing after they get started. The result? Sleepless nights worrying about where the next check is coming from. Missed opportunities and—potentially—an addition to the SBA failure rate statistics.

Failure, by the way, is a relative term. Believe it or not, it's something you as an entrepreneur shouldn't allow yourself to become paralyzed by avoiding. Actually, relatively few businesses close from abject financial failure (i.e., bankruptcy or insolvency). But many entrepreneurs found failure—often more than once—before hitting the right combination of circumstances that resulted in success. So don't let the possibility of failure get in the way of taking charge of your life.

Back to the money. How do you escape these two money fallacies? How do you realistically estimate how much money you really need? Depending on the nature of your goals, there are two different ways to determine how much money you'll need both to get your business started and to keep it going. The first one's easy and works just fine for most people.

BACK OF THE ENVELOPE

This is the quick-and-dirty way to estimate what it will take to get your business off the ground, and it's the approach Peter used in starting his own home-based writing business. He didn't spend night after night putting together a fifty-page business plan. That seems to be what's advocated in most every how-to-start-a-business book you'll ever read, but for the vast majority of people who want to start their own businesses, the business plan becomes nothing more than a great big obstacle on the path to success.

So Peter didn't do a twelve-month estimate of cash flow, and he didn't put together a complex, multilayered budget on his computer. He simply took some time to think about what things he would need to make his business happen and then to determine how much money would be required to purchase items he didn't already have.

As it turned out, Peter's family, like most households today, already had a computer and a printer. Those were two big things he could quickly cross off his list. He already had an Internet account with America Online, so that cost was already covered. His employer (Peter started his business while he was still working in a full-time position for a local government agency) paid for health care and other benefits for him and his family. He also had already purchased a nice used office desk and task chair from a previous employer for pennies on the dollar.

Peter could create his own business cards on his laser printer and cut them by hand. A box of printer paper, a few pens, a stapler, and a roll of tape would keep him well supplied for quite some time. The only thing he really needed to purchase that involved any significant outlay of funds was a wireless telephone to make and receive business calls when he was away from the office. And make calls he did, as that was a low-cost way to line up business.

In other words, as most people who want to create their own job discover, Peter was ready and able to start his business without much money at all. His business start-up was already mostly paid for, and a simple, back-of-the-envelope calculation was all he needed to get his business off and running. The biggest costs for him and for most people who go out on their own are their ongoing living expenses. So this has to be part of your calculations.

How much do you need to live on?

How much can you get by with?

How much do you hope for?

How much of this do others provide?

The good news for Peter was that, because he started his business while holding down a full-time job, he already had a steady source of cash coming in to pay his living expenses. These expenses included a house payment, car payments, food, utilities, and the other essentials of life today, and it would have been a significant challenge for Peter and his family to get by without the income (and benefits) from a full-time job as he started up his business and slowly built a client base.

Once the business was going, Peter created a spreadsheet on his computer to track his incoming cash from clients (technically, this is known as *accounts receivable*) and his expenses *(accounts payable)*—both business and personal—by project, by month. This spreadsheet—which Peter maintains religiously to this day—helps him anticipate times when payments might be few and far between and money therefore tight, so he can make his plans accordingly.

So, before you spend hours and hours getting over the hurdle of preparing full-blown sales and expense estimates—or, heaven forbid, a complicated and unnecessary formal business plan—see whether you can get by with this back-of-the-

---

SELLING STUFF TO START UP

Todd Smart raised the money to buy the first tow truck for his business—southern California–based Absolute Towing and Trucking—by selling his car. Within ten years of starting his business, annual sales climbed to $5 million.

To finance his start-up company—TriNet Communications, Inc., in Livermore, California—founder Jon Fernandez sold a rental house he owned for $50,000.

envelope approach. If so, you'll find yourself out on your own sooner than you ever thought possible.

Key Question: Has the thought of having to write a business plan for your new business stopped you from actually starting it? If so, remember: The majority of small businesses do not need a business plan to get started. Instead, the best thing to do is often to just do it. The key is to be always moving forward toward your goal and to refuse to allow obstacles like this to get in your way. Before you go to bed each night, set at least one goal to accomplish the next day that brings you closer to starting your own business. Write it down in a notebook, and then when you accomplish it, cross it off your list.

THE BIG GUNS

But perhaps you have grand plans for your business. Maybe you plan to go for a loan. Or, like Stuart Wilde of Wilde Llama Adventures, you need to buy four llamas and several acres of land to get your business going. If that's the case, then the informal, back-of-the-envelope approach won't be sufficient. To gain an accurate picture of your financial needs, it's time to bring out the big guns. You'll need to take a formal look at three things in detail: your projected sales, your projected start-up costs, and your projected recurring costs. But don't let that become an obstacle. In plain English, here's what you do.

Project Your Sales

Sales are the top line of your business—the income that keeps your business going, provides your living expenses, and hopefully results in profit that you can use to expand and improve your business. As you'll soon find out, the more sales you've got, the merrier.

BOOTSTRAPPING

When partners Elan Susser and Jon Ferrara founded their business—GoldMine Software—they only had $5,000 taken from Ferrara's savings to fund the start-up. Not only were funds few and far between, but so was their experience with running a business—they had none.

Instead of seeking other sources of funding and going into debt, Susser and Ferrara decided to *bootstrap* their business—that is, grow the business on whatever revenues it produced. This meant their business could only grow as much and as fast as profits would allow.

In the beginning, Susser and Ferrara lived and worked in a cheap apartment, took little or no salary, and ate a *lot* of macaroni and cheese. To keep themselves motivated, they placed a postcard with a panoramic view of the Santa Monica coast on their office refrigerator. Recalls Ferrara, "Every day, when we'd go reheat our macaroni and cheese, we'd look at it and visualize it as the view from our future office."

The company was a success. Today, GoldMine is one of the top contact management software products. And it didn't take long for

Here's how to project your sales: Estimate how much business you can expect to do in the first month. You can do this by determining exactly who is going to buy something from you—contacts you've already lined up—and making a guess as to *when* they will actually buy and *how much* they will buy. Each business is different, and different businesses have different selling cycles; while one business may generate immediate sales, another business may require a significant investment of time and relationship building before sales start to build. How much

venture capitalists and investment bankers to start lining up for a piece of the pie. But Susser and Ferrara didn't bite. They preferred to stick with the bootstrap strategy that had brought them so far. Says Susser, "We were worried about outside people funding the company and dictating its direction. We preferred to wake up in the morning and make our own decisions."

About ten years after founding their company, Susser and Ferrara still retained a 90 percent ownership stake in the company, and, when GoldMine was eventually merged with a competitor, the two partners emerged with $83 million and a significant minority stake in the combined firm.

Although it took longer to reach their goals, Ferrara believes that theirs was the right approach. "It took us five years to become a serious company," says Ferrara. "If we had funding, it would have taken us one or two years. But because we created the company on our own revenue stream, we were forced to do things intelligently and profitably from the beginning."

do you expect to sell in your second and third months? Project your monthly sales for an entire year.

"But," you say, "I don't know." Of course you don't know. You're guessing. Hopefully it's an educated guess based on what you learned by researching when you decided to start the kind of business you selected or by speaking with others who are already well established in that kind of business.

When Sarah started her private psychotherapy practice, for example, she estimated that based on the contacts and referral

---

Raging Success

Bill Martin and Greg Wright started their company—Raging Bull—with a total of $175: $75 to pay for a New Jersey partnership fee, $70 to register their Web domain name, and $30 for the first month of their Web hosting service. Because they were both college students, they were able to receive free use of their schools' high-speed, T1 Internet lines—an "in-kind" service worth thousands of dollars a month to the business. Bill and Greg's business, which built a virtual community of people interested in the stock market, did so well that it soon attracted a $2 million investment from the venture capital firm @Ventures.

---

sources she had and the few clients she could take with her from the center where she worked, which was closing, she could attract four clients in the first month and another four each month until by the end of the year, accounting for attrition, she planned to have a full practice with twenty-six clients a week.

Did she guess right? No. It took six months longer than she expected. So she supplemented her income by filling in at a university counseling center for several months until she hit her projections.

Decide what you will charge. "Eeek! What? How would I do this?" you may wonder. Don't fret. Many people don't have a clue what they can charge when they start out. Again, it will be an educated guess. For example, as a newcomer to the area but with strong clinical experience, Sarah guessed she would be able to charge midrange of what other therapists in the area were charging. And how did she get that figure? By asking other therapists what the going rate was and by asking people she knew who were already in therapy what they were used to paying.

Create a computer spreadsheet that lays out your sales estimates for the entire year. How certain do you feel about each individual number? Discount your numbers by the amount of uncertainty you feel. So, for example, if you feel that a particular sale next month to a good friend named Susan is an absolute certainty—after all, she promised that she would buy the items from you—then multiply it by 100 percent (thereby giving this particular sale full credit). If, however, you feel that a sale next month is kind of iffy—it was only a vague expression of interest from a friend of a friend named Max—then factor it accordingly, perhaps multiplying it by 50 percent to reduce its value in half. This guesswork would look something like this:

Projected January Sales: Sandy Beach Enterprises

Susan:	$500 × 1.00 =	$500
Max:	$500 × 0.50 =	$250
Total:		$750

Total your monthly figures to determine your total projected sales for the year.

Project Your Start-Up Costs

Like any new enterprise, you'll have certain costs, necessary as a part of starting up, that will recur infrequently if ever again. Remember: Unless you're really clever, you're going to spend this money *before* you receive a dime from your prospective customers and clients! Some of these costs include things like these:

Permits and licenses

Professional fees pertaining to business start-up (e.g., a
    lawyer hired to incorporate your business)

Deposits for rent, insurance coverage, and other needs

Furniture, office equipment, and supplies

Beginning inventory

Project Your Recurring Costs

Every business also has certain expenses that must be paid on a regular basis—the costs that are a result of normal operations, just as you have ongoing expenses for rent, house payments, food, electricity, and so forth in your personal life. For a business, these expenses—known as *recurring costs*—include payments for things such as these:

Wages, salaries, and benefits (This includes your wages. Your salary and benefits may be your only payroll costs at first or as a one-person business, forever.)

Rent

Utilities

Insurance

Inventory

Internet access

Telephones

Loan payments

Leases for office equipment

Taxes

"But," you say, "how much do I pay myself?" Unfortunately, for most self-employed business owners, the answer to that is however much is left over after you've fed the business—and that's often not very much at all. Don't make that mistake. Build.

Add It All Up

Based on the prior information, you can quickly determine how much money you'll need for the first year of your business. Start with your projected sales for the year, and then subtract your start-up costs and your recurring costs. The amount of money remaining is how much profit you'll make for the year (or, if you're losing money, how much you'll need to come up with during the course of the year, remembering that you'll have to come up with your projected start-up costs *before* you start selling to clients and customers). Here's an example:

First-Year Financials: Sandy Beach Enterprises

Projected sales:	$15,000
Projected start-up costs:	($ 5,000)
Projected recurring costs:	($ 7,500)
Total:	$ 2,500

In this example, the owner of Sandy Beach Enterprises is going to make $2,500 profit after considering the money she takes into the business (sales) and the money she sends out of the business (costs). If her sales had been $5,000 less, however ($10,000 instead of $15,000), she would have *lost* $2,500 for that year. Either way, the money to start up the business doesn't come out of thin air; it must come from personal resources or from outside sources of funds. We'll take a closer look at these sources of money in the next section.

Question 2:
How Much Do I *Really* Have?

We bet you have more than you think. The most popular source of cash by far for people starting up their own businesses is from personal sources. In fact, according to a recent survey of the five hundred fastest-growing small businesses conducted by *Inc.* magazine, personal assets were the *primary* source of start-up capital, at 92 percent of those companies polled.

> The most popular source of cash by far for people starting up their own businesses is from personal sources.

The advantages of using personal sources of cash are that they are often quick and easy to obtain compared to getting cash from someone else who you will need to pay back. If you've got a couple of hundred bucks in your savings account, for example, you can probably get your hands on it pretty quickly—and you won't have to fill out a ten-page application form to get it!

The disadvantages of personal sources of cash are that they may be limited (few of us have $5,000 or $10,000 just sitting around gathering dust!), and their use may jeopardize the stability of your own personal financial situation. For example, if you siphon $5,000 off your own salaried income to start your own business, you may stretch yourself so thin financially that you suddenly have a hard time making your mortgage payments or paying for other routine personal expenses. That's why a careful analysis of your own financial obligations and what you need to live is so important.

Take a good look at the resources you have access to. Here are some of the most common personal sources of cash. Which ones of these do you have or could you create? We think you'll be surprised.

Day job

Nest egg

Plastic

Home sweet home loans

I scratch your back; you scratch mine

Money later

Money up front

In kind

DAY JOB

For many people starting their own business—and looking for the cash they need to start it—a day job makes for a really nice piggy bank. Whether it's a full- or part-time job, many people use income from their salaries to get started. And, if money is tight, instead of going on vacation or going out to eat, they'll funnel any extra money they've got into their new business. Still others do temp work to get their businesses started and to keep them going. And, don't forget: You can adjust your paycheck tax withholdings as a way to free up extra money to start your business—the fewer withholdings you take, the more money you'll take home in each paycheck. Have a chat with your payroll department to get the forms you'll need to make the change.

NEST EGG

Do you have a savings account? If so, you've got a ready-made source of cash to fund your business. Depending on how much money you've got in your account, you can draw down your entire account—or just a portion—to fund your business start-up and operations. Once your business gets off the ground and starts making a profit, then you can pay back your savings account.

PLASTIC

Credit cards are a key source of business funding. It's rare to speak with a successful business owner who has not at one time or another turned to his or her personal credit cards to fund the start-up phase of a business or to keep the enterprise afloat when expenses were high or business was slow. If your credit is good, you've probably already got several credit cards you can use to obtain cash advances or to buy equipment and supplies. For most purposes, credit cards are as good as cash. Just don't forget that at some point you're going to have to pay back your credit card company! And credit card interest rates are high, so it's best to use credit cards for purchases that will bring in income (e.g., a printer you can print marketing materials with) rather than to cover living expenses or to buy new filing cabinets.

HOME SWEET HOME LOANS

Do you own your home? Does your home have equity (the positive difference between how much your home is worth and how much money you owe the bank)? If so, then you are literally sitting on a gold mine. With a home equity loan or home equity line of credit, you can obtain a loan that is based on the equity in your home. What's more, interest rates for home equity loans are often very favorable, and you may be able to deduct your interest from your income taxes.

If you've got lots of equity, the amount of money available to you can be quite substantial, and you may be able to obtain it relatively quickly. The downside is that, in exchange for the loan, your mortgage payments will be higher until such time as the loan is paid off and retired. Also, if you get behind on your payments, you risk foreclosure and losing your home.

If you can refinance your home for a lower interest rate, however, you may be able to keep your payments virtually the same and still take money out for your business. Sort of like having your cake and eating it too.

So talk to your lender. Talk to a variety of lenders. Compare what kind of deal you can get.

I Scratch Your Back; You Scratch Mine

What products or services could you provide in exchange for someone else providing you with the services you need to start your business? Such barter arrangements enable you to get aspects of your business under way without cash. *Barter* simply means trading some of your products or services in return for someone else's. If, for example, you're planning to start a house-painting business, and you need the help of a CPA to get your accounting system set up, perhaps you could trade some of your painting services to the CPA in return for some of his services.

A Barter Example

The founders of Bridgepath.com—an Internet exchange for permanent and temporary staffing firms, located in San Francisco—were committed to financing their business with their own resources and to not taking on debts or turning to outside loans. To do this, they used barter to exchange services with vendors in lieu of making cash payments. Specifically, they asked employees to bring spare furniture to work to furnish their offices (thus keeping the cost of furnishing each office under $50), negotiated with four different long-distance telephone companies to get the very best deal (saving thousands of dollars in charges), and convinced vendors to accept delayed payments.

The great thing about barter is that you don't need cash to obtain products and services you need. The bad thing is that it may be difficult to find someone who is willing to trade what you need for what you've got to offer. To help get around this problem, barter exchanges have sprung up in some communities to bring together people who have products or services to trade. There are also a number of associations of professional barterers that cater to businesses that conduct very large barter transactions. Here are just a few places to go for further information:

- Continental Trade Exchange: www.ctebarter.com
- International Reciprocal Trade Association: www.irta.com
- ITEX International Trade Exchange: www.ubarter.com
- National Association of Trade Exchanges: www.nate.org
- TradeAway: www.tradeaway.com

Money Later

Traditionally, many businesses sell their products to other businesses on credit, with payment expected thirty days after purchase (or thirty days after receipt of an invoice). When a company gives you "net/30" payment terms like these, this amounts to a free loan to your company for thirty days. In another example of such trade credit, you may retail products for another company—say, vacuum cleaners—and not be required to pay your vendor until you sell the item. If the consigned item is not sold, you can send it back to your vendor without ever having paid a dime. Not too shabby, eh?

Money Up Front

If you've ever hired a construction company to remodel your home or build a pool in your backyard, you know that few companies will pick up a shovel without being paid at least half of the construction price in advance. There are a number of benefits to this approach of billing customers before you actually perform the work.

First, you have the use of the money from your customer from the time you deposit the check in the bank until you finally spend the last dollar on expenses to complete the job. Not only that, but you've got the security of knowing that you will be paid at least for that portion of the job. While most customers and clients are ethical and will pay you when you complete your work or deliver your product, there are exceptions—and it only takes a few exceptions to put you out of business.

Sometimes you can also get paid on installments. If, for example, you have a large project, you can get partial payment up front and intermittent payments at prearranged intervals. If you can line up such projects before leaving your job, this is an ideal way to ease into a business.

In Kind

Money isn't really what you need. You need money so you can buy what you need. What if you didn't have to buy the things you need? What if you could get people to loan or give them to you or to simply volunteer to do them for you?

Question 3: How Can I Get More If There's a Gap?

So, what are you supposed to do if you've figured out how much money you need for the start-up phase and operations, and you've closely examined your personal resources, but you've come up short? It means it's time to look for outside sources of cash. Here are some of the most common outside sources of cash:

Making a B&B Dream Come True

Linda Madden Miller dreamed of having a bed and breakfast in the mountain community in which she lived. She was living in a small home with her husband and son when a large home with suitable zoning came on the market. With no capital, she had no obvious way to buy the house and spend the $15,000 to $50,000 per guest room the Professional Innkeepers Association of America has found it costs to renovate a property. And she certainly didn't have the $10,000 per room working capital for utilities, insurance, marketing, maintenance, and supplies the association recommends.

Linda did her homework. She stayed at a B&B in a different market and asked questions. She told her friends what she wanted to do, and they shared her enthusiasm in large part because they had confidence in Linda's ability to make a B&B a "go" and wanted to be a part of it.

Four of them invested $5,000 each. Others donated furnishings like kitchenware, tableware, heirloom china, furniture, draperies, area rugs, lamps, sofa, bedding and sheets, towels, and knickknacks. Much of what she got were "family items" not in use but dear enough to be held in storage. Linda had to turn away some things and donate others to charities.

Fans

Bankers

Partners

Uncle Sam

Angels

Capitalists

Five friends took on decorating the four bedrooms at no cost to Linda. Each decorator chose a theme for her room. Linda said she trusted them to "shut the door and do their thing." Her handy husband handled needed repairs and carpentry.

The total cash outlay, including the down payment on the house, covering all furnishing and decorating, amounted to $23,000. Her marketing costs were kept low, forgoing expensive display advertising in favor of going to all kinds of meetings—community, school district, chamber of commerce, church, and merchant—and relying on word-of-mouth advertising developed by guests.

For radio advertising, she bartered gift certificates for weekends at the B&B for use in radio station contests. She also bartered weekend stays at the B&B for propane, a top for the spa, housecleaning, and an antique armoire.

Linda believes she was able to do all this by "not thinking you can't do it" and instead letting herself be creative while working within a budget.

The advantage of outside sources of cash is that they can far exceed the amount of cash you can raise from personal sources. Not only that but, by using other people's money, you can avoid putting your own money at risk.

The disadvantage of outside sources of cash is that, when you accept the money, you create an obligation to someone else, whether it is to a friend, bank, partner, or other investor. In some cases, you may need to give up a significant portion of your ownership stake in the company in exchange for the cash you need, introducing the possibility that someone may attempt to take over your business or, at minimum, push his or her own agenda. Finally, of course, you have to find these investors and convince them to part with their money, something most people don't do easily.

> You never know exactly who will give you the money you need until you ask.

Whether you can do this or not depends on who you are, who you know, what you've done, and what you're proposing. Before you decide you don't know anyone who would give you the money you need or that you certainly wouldn't qualify for a loan or other, more formal source of cash, think again—you may be surprised. You never know exactly who will give you the money you need until you ask.

FANS

So, who do you know who really thinks you are the best thing going? Who believes in you enough to loan, advance, or outright give you the money you need? Often, when personal sources of funds are insufficient to support the start-up and operation of a business, people turn first to friends and family before they go to other sources.

Do you have a rich uncle with some spare cash on his hands? Or perhaps a successful friend who is looking for new business ventures in which to invest her money? Maybe a colleague who thinks the world really needs your business idea? If so, you've got a potential source for the money you need to get your business off the ground and running.

$100,000 FOR THE ASKING

Lewis Cirne, founder of Wily Technology, asked family friends to help finance his Santa Cruz, California, home-based software development business. Says Lewis, "I raised $35,000 from friends of my parents—they each kicked in five grand. When I had my big idea, I sent them a ten-page e-mail document, and they sent in the money. There was real pressure because, although they weren't my family, they were friends of my family." Lewis raised another sizable chunk of money—$65,000—by approaching his friends, including his former school headmaster.

If you do decide to accept money from friends and family, however, that you and they intend for you to pay back (i.e., it's not a gift), be sure that you set up the transaction as a formal loan, with a written loan agreement and an agreed-to rate of interest and payment schedule. Nothing can turn a relationship sour faster than money problems; treating money from family and friends as a formal loan will help you avoid misunderstandings and other problems.

> Treating money from family and friends as a formal loan will help you avoid misunderstandings and other problems.

BANKERS

Banks and credit unions are the traditional places many entrepreneurs look to for outside sources of cash to fund their businesses. Understand, however, that most banks are wary of lending to new businesspeople who lack a track record of

---

A LOAN FOR SECURITY

Michael Knowles founded Tallahassee, Florida–based Seven Hills Security, Inc., in his home with $1,000 borrowed from a friend. The business has since grown to more than 130 employees and $2.1 million in annual revenues.

---

financial success. Outside of professional practices, such as doctors and accountants, they aren't eager to loan money for one-person enterprises. Not many writers, for example, get a bank loan to write the Great American Novel. As the common refrain among savvy entrepreneurs goes, "A banker is someone who lends you an umbrella when the sun shines and who wants it back when it starts to rain."

If you decide to request a loan from your bank or credit union, the SBA suggests you prepare a written loan proposal. Here, according to the SBA, are the key components of a well-written loan proposal:

- *General information.* Be sure to include (1) the business name, names of principals, the Social Security number for each principal, and the business address; (2) the purpose of the loan—exactly what the loan will be used for and why it is needed; and (3) the amount required—the exact amount you need to achieve your purpose.
- *Business description.* Cite (1) the history and nature of the business—details of what kind of business it is, its age, number of employees, and current business assets; and (2) ownership structure—details on your company's legal structure.
- *Management profile.* Develop a short statement on each principal in your business; provide their background, education, experience, skills, and accomplishments.

- *Market information.* (1) Clearly define your company's products as well as your markets; (2) identify your competition and explain how your business competes in the marketplace; and (3) profile your customers, noting how your business can satisfy their needs.

- *Financial information.* Include (1) financial statements—balance sheets and income statements for the past three years (if you are starting out, provide a projected balance sheet and income statement); (2) personal financial statements on yourself and other principal owners of the business; and (3) collateral you would be willing to pledge as security for the loan.

If you find that conventional loans are available to you, you might want to explore whether you'd be eligible for a microloan or some other form of government funding. (See the section "Uncle Sam.") Not sure if you'd qualify for a loan or where to begin finding a lender? Visit Quicken Loans at http://quicken-loans.quicken.com/. Not only will you find out about many of

---

MICROLOAN, MACROGROWTH

When Luisa Hechavarrias of Denver, Colorado, dreamed of starting her own business, she wanted one that would allow her to stay at home and keep an eye on her three kids. Luisa started her business—Friendly Auto Glass—with a $2,000 microloan that she received from the Colorado National Bank Community Enterprise Lending Initiative (CELI) program. Luisa was able to leverage this small financial stake into a very successful enterprise. According to Luisa, "It's lucrative; I can see the growth. If I keep at it, I'll eventually be able to save for the future and for my children."

THE FINANCIAL SIX Cs

If you find that you need to seek a loan to put together sufficient funds to start your business, you should know about the Six Cs, the qualities that banks and other lenders look for in borrowers as a part of the loan process. While you may not need to score a hundred points on each C, obviously, the more points the merrier. Here are each of the Cs—do you measure up?

- *Character.* The degree to which a borrower feels a moral obligation to pay his or her debts, measured by his or her credit history. Consistent, on-time payments over a long period of time are good; consistent late payments or bankruptcy are bad.
- *Capacity to pay.* A subjective determination made by a lender based on an analysis of the borrower's financial statements and other information. Is your business going to generate sufficient cash flow to keep up with the payments required for a loan in the amount you've requested? If so, you'll do well here. If not, you'll be asked to scale back your request.

the loan possibilities available to you and review current interest rates for different kinds of loans, but you'll also be able to use a variety of loan calculators to find out exactly which loans you'll qualify for, and how much money you can expect to obtain.

PARTNERS

You may want to invite someone to join you in your venture and share ownership for a variety of reasons. You can share

- *Capital.* The amount of capital in a business is the amount of cash available from both debt and equity. Lenders prefer low debt-to-asset and debt-to-worth ratios and high current ratios (measures of the amount of debt you carry vs. the amount of cash and other assets your business possesses). These indicate financial stability.
- *Collateral.* An asset owned by the borrower, but promised to a lender against nonpayment of the loan. The amount of collateral required varies from lender to lender and from loan to loan. The closer the value of the collateral is to the amount of the loan requested, the more comfortable the lender will be loaning you the money you need.
- *Conditions.* The general conditions of the economy at the time, as well as industry trends. A strong economy frees up more capital for loans; a weak economy makes capital harder to find.
- *Confidence.* The overall picture of the prospective borrower that the lender gets by reviewing the preceding five Cs. If the borrower's answers to these Cs are strong, then a lender's confidence will be high, and the requested loan will likely be funded. If a lender's confidence is low, then the requested loan will likely be turned down.

expenses, of course, but perhaps your partner has expertise you lack and would otherwise have to pay considerable amounts to hire or purchase. Maybe your partner is a better salesperson or businessperson than you, so he or she could bring in more clients more quickly. Likewise, maybe your partner has better contacts with potential customers or with prospective vendors than you. Or perhaps you just need his or her contribution of cash or moral support.

Whatever the case, don't jump lightly into a partnership. When they are good, partnerships can be very, very good, but when they are bad, they are horrid. Be as careful in bringing a partner into your business as you would be in choosing a mate. You can run into problems when partners disagree on the direction of the company or when one partner flakes out or tries to take over. If you decide to partner, be sure to have a written partnership agreement that spells out exactly what will happen if one partner wants to buy the other out or if the business is dissolved. And keep in mind that, as a partnership, *you* will be legally liable for anything your partner does in conjunction with the business (and vice versa).

> Be as careful in bringing a partner into your business as you would be in choosing a mate.

UNCLE SAM

The government—specifically, the Small Business Administration—has a long history of encouraging the formation and growth of businesses by way of a variety of financing programs. Why? Because small businesses provide approximately 75 percent of new jobs in the United States, and they develop 55 percent of the country's innovations.

The SBA actually doesn't provide the cash for the commonly used "SBA loans" that you've probably heard so much about. The agency instead acts to guarantee the loans made by banks and other approved private sector lenders—more than $12 billion worth in fiscal year 2000. Because the loans are guaranteed by the government, lenders are much more willing to loan money to applicants who might not normally qualify.

Even so, to qualify for a loan like this, you'll still need to have a good credit history, some collateral to put up against the loan, and a winning business plan. Unfortunately, not every business—or aspiring entrepreneur—can make the grade, and many go away empty-handed.

That's where the SBA's microloan program comes in.

Microloans are loans in the range of $100 to $35,000 (with an average loan amount of about $10,500) funded by the SBA and distributed by local, community-based nonprofit organizations called *intermediaries.* Loan proceeds are generally limited to the purchase of supplies, inventory, equipment, furniture, machinery and use as working capital—that is, cash on hand to pay the bills. The great thing about microloans is that they are much easier to qualify for than most any other kind of loan, and funds can be obtained very quickly, often within a week after an application is submitted.

> The great thing about microloans is that they are much easier to qualify for than most any other kind of loan, and funds can be obtained very quickly, often within a week after an application is submitted.

After spending years as a plumber's apprentice and working for someone else, Lori Miceli—owner of Lori K. Mechanical, Inc., a plumbing business located in Vincentown, New Jersey—was determined to start her own business. In a field traditionally dominated by men, Lori had to work extra hard to make her dream come true. Turning to the New Jersey Authority for Small Businesses, Minorities' and Women's Enterprises, she received help in exploring financing options and writing a business plan. Using her business plan, Lori obtained a microloan in the amount of $25,000 from Trenton

---

KEY RESOURCES

For more information on microloans, including a list of intermediaries in your area, be sure to check out the SBA microloan site at www .sba.gov/financing/frmicro.html.

Business Assistance Corporation (TBAC), an SBA microloan intermediary. Without this loan, she would have had a very difficult time getting her business off the ground.

"Being a female contractor in the construction industry, I found it tough getting my foot in the door and getting started," Lori says. "Finding financing is also difficult. With the help of the Entrepreneurial Training Institute and a loan from TBAC, I was able to get established, support myself, and build my business reputation." Lori K. Mechanical, Inc., is a success, and the company continues to grow—Lori subsequently received a $75,000 SBA-guaranteed line of credit from a local bank.

Frequently people ask us about grants for starting a business, sometimes because TV commercials selling seminars and books say there's free money out there. If you're a member of a minority group, live in a rural area, or have a disability, you may be able to get grant money. To the extent such funds are available, they're administered by either state agencies, regional public bodies, or nonprofit corporations serving residents in their areas. One way to find out about who administers funds in your area is to contact your state representative or senator; another is to search your state's Web site.

As you can see, grants are neither readily available nor easy to get. Thus, most people start a business by bootstrapping, tightening their living expenses, turning to savings, lining up business in advance, or cajoling loans from family and friends.

ANGELS

Angels are private individuals with a healthy net worth who invest in a start-up or growing business for fun and profit. Indeed, for many entrepreneurs, angels are truly heaven-sent. While you may not be familiar with the impact that angel investors are having on business today, it is *huge.* According to the SBA, more than 250,000 angel investors in the United States are pumping more than $20 billion into over 30,000 small firms a year. And, while a decade ago the average individual investment for angel investors was between $48,000 and $60,000, today that figure has grown to $145,000.

> According to the SBA, more than 250,000 angel investors in the United States are pumping more than $20 billion into over 30,000 small firms a year.

The best way to meet angel investors is by networking through friends and business acquaintances (lawyers and doctors are well-known sources of angel investors) or by schmoozing at industry events or chamber of commerce meetings. Access to Capital Electronic Network (Ace-Net) matches angels and entrepreneurs. You can find this group on the Web at http://ace -net.sr.unh.edu.

Key Questions: Afraid to ask for money? Ask yourself this: If you had the money, what kind of approach would persuade you to invest in someone else's venture? Enthusiasm? Confidence? Good numbers? A logical approach?

If that works for you, who do you know or might you meet who thinks that way? Try this approach to telling your story, because practicing will help: Make your case in front of

FEEDING A RESTAURANT DREAM WITH FRIENDS' MONEY

When Duke Rohlen and high school friend Maurice Werdegar decided to join together in 1993 to found their Palo Alto, California–based restaurant Blue Chalk Café, they knew they would need money—and a lot of it. They also knew that, because the restaurant was not yet in business—and therefore had no track record of success—no bank would loan them the money they would need to get their venture off the ground.

So, instead of filling out application forms and wasting time hanging out in bank lobbies, they decided to approach their fans—family and friends—for the money they needed. The two partners approached every person they knew who they believed could afford to purchase a $12,500 stake in the business. According to Duke Rohlen, "We priced it so that people could afford to have a token investment. If they lost, it was still fun to have been involved in owning a restaurant."

To bolster their case with potential investors, they created a full-blown business plan that supported the wisdom of the investment. Still, people weren't exactly knocking down their doors to buy the $12,500 stakes in the business-to-be. Says Duke, "First, why would anyone want to invest in a restaurant—they have a high failure rate—and, second, why should they give money to novices?" Neither had ever before started up or owned a restaurant.

a mirror, or videotape your presentation. Then try it on someone you know.

CAPITALISTS

Venture capitalists (VCs) are people who make money available in exchange for a major stake in the ownership of a grow-

What put their business idea on the map, however, was an open house that the partners held at the historic building in which they planned to operate their restaurant. According to Duke, "We invited all the potential investors to the Blue Chalk Café space and served bagels and orange juice, so people could see the charm of the building. People liked that. It was tangible." The result? The two entrepreneurs raised $600,000, enough to open the doors of their new venture.

Only a year later, the Blue Chalk Café was bringing in more than $3 million a year in sales, and the successful duo was busy raising money for their Left at Albuquerque restaurant concept (springboarding on the success of the Blue Chalk Café, they quickly raised another $900,000).

Reflecting on his success, Duke Rohlen realizes that he and his partner would never have made it without the help of family and friends, and he also realizes that he and his partner felt a special obligation in accepting their money. "When we were asking for money," he says, "we were young, and a lot of our friends that we approached didn't have a lot of disposable income. Even $12,500 was a lot. It really motivates you to succeed when you think about losing a friend's or a family member's investment."

ing firm, and venture capital was the engine that drove the recent explosion of dot-coms (and the subsequent withdrawal of it accompanied the even more recent *implosion* of dot-coms). Let's start with the bad news about VCs: Fewer than 1 percent of all businesses meet their strict requirements. This means that, chances are, venture capital is not going to be a realistic source of outside funding for you and your firm. If, however, you are within that small group of firms that are attractive to VCs, you may be able to receive a substantial amount of cash to pump into your business in exchange for an ownership stake in your business.

Keep in mind that before approaching angels and venture capitalists you need a well-thought-out business and financial plan that has believable milestones for growing your business. To learn more about angels and venture capital, we recommend *Raising Capital for Dummies* by venture capital expert Joe Bartlett and Peter Economy.

Key Questions: Did you already know about these financial resources? If so, have you explored them fully? If not, ask yourself, "What's been keeping me from pursuing them?" If that's where you're stuck, don't think results at this point; think curiosity. What would happen if you applied for a loan? Or for another loan? What might happen if you pulled together some colleagues and friends for a fund-raising brainstorming session? And so on. What might you discover that could lead you to the answer you've been missing?

Question 4: How Can I Start with What I've Got?

Now comes the moment of truth. You know how much money you need to start and operate your business. You know how much money you have. You know whether you need more money, and you know how you could get it. That's your reality. That's your situation. Now you get to figure out how to proceed with whatever you can create.

If you've got what you need, you're ready to go. If not, go back over your personal resources. Review your sources of outside cash. Have you exhausted them all? If so, go back and take another look at your money figures. Do you really need that much cash to get started? Maybe not. Take a very serious look at what you need and see whether you can get by with less.

Maybe the simple fact is that you can't start as big as you'd like or as soon as you'd like. Maybe you'll have to keep your day job and start out small-time on the side (not a bad idea, as far as we're concerned). Maybe, like Stuart Wilde, you'll have to work as a part-time cook while you get things going. Maybe you'll need more time to line up the financial support you need.

Wherever you find yourself financially, you are not stuck unless you choose to be. Now you simply have to do whatever it is you need to do next, and you will have gotten past the money obstacle that's been hanging you up.

So, at this point, ask yourself:

What can I do now?

Not what do you *wish* you could do. Or what you *hope* to do. But what you actually *can* do now. Then do it. And keep moving ahead based on what you discover. Refuse to let what seems like a lack of money become a life-

> Millions of people have gotten past this obstacle by doing whatever it is they can do right now.

long obstacle. Millions of people have gotten past this obstacle by doing whatever it is they can do right now. And so can you! Just keep asking . . .

What can *I do now?*

Our Bias

After all is said and done about obtaining outside money, we have to admit that we have a bias. Whenever possible, we

---

AUCTIONING FOR PROFIT

Terri Cook is a stay-at-home mom who financed her business—Net Auctions Software, a seller of low-cost educational software on the auction Web site eBay.com—with the money she made selling her very first products. Says Terri, "In the very beginning I was successful, which was why I got hooked so quickly. The first item I sold was a book that I purchased at a garage sale for 25 cents—it sold for over $38! I sold about a dozen items like that and thought that I'd found a gold mine." Besides requiring very little money to get her business off the ground, Terri enjoys other aspects as well. "I love the flexibility that online auctions offer. I can work when my kids are sleeping or busy with something else. I can take vacations at anytime. It's a stay-at-home mother's dream!"

---

believe the safest and surest way to get a business going—especially a one-person business in which *you're* the business—is by doing as Elan Susser and Jon Ferrara, founders of GoldMine Software, did: Bootstrap your business.

Bootstrapping your business means building it based on whatever revenues it produces and not overextending yourself with loans and other outside sources of cash. This way your business grows only as much and as fast and as far as the profits allow. This keeps your feet on the ground and assures you don't get ahead of yourself and fall on your face. You may trip, but you won't fall.

Of course, bootstrapping is the method of necessity for anyone who cannot qualify for loans, those whose personal sources of funding are tapped out, and those who simply want to conserve their precious cash and stretch it as far as possible.

Here are our three golden rules of bootstrapping:

- *Rule 1: Hire as few employees as possible.* When you're starting your new business, the old truism "hire slow, fire fast" really makes sense. Employees—with their wages, benefits, and other expenses—are usually the most expensive thing that businesses spend their money on. Avoid the urge to hire employees unless it's absolutely necessary. A much better alternative is to hire independent professionals (say, for example, a part-time bookkeeper). Not only will you not have to pay all the extra expenses that come along with employees, but it's far easier to tell an independent professional you no longer need his or her services than it is to tell an employee he or she is fired.

- *Rule 2: Lease, share, and barter everything you can.* There are some things that almost every business needs—a computer, a printer, a desk, chairs, office space—and you may believe that you'll need to shell out a lot of cash to get your business set up. This is definitely not the case. Instead of paying $1,500 for a new computer and printer, you can lease one for $15 a month (tax-deductible, of course). Instead of running out to buy a desk and chairs, you can barter your services to get what you need from a business that has more than it needs. Instead of signing a two-year lease for office space, you can beg a friend to let you use an extra office in her building (or you can simply take over that spare bedroom down the hall).

- *Rule 3: Get money up front.* Remember: It is almost always better to use money from the people who will owe it to you than to use your own to fuel your business. Have your customers pay you in advance for work that you agree to do for them or for products you sell to them. Arrange progress payments. Request net/30 terms from your vendors so you have the benefit of using their money for a month or more before you have to pay your bills. Be stingy; hold on to your money as long as you possibly can!

Once again from the issues and information in this chapter, identify three things you want or need to do. Write them down in the Personal Action Plan in Appendix A: Take-Off Section, beginning on page 294.

CHAPTER FIVE

I Don't Know the Nitty-Gritty of Starting a Business

I don't know anything at all about business—how can I get one started?

How do I attract enough customers to make money?

I'm not any good with numbers—how will I keep track of my money?

I've already read a lot of books on starting a business—is there a better way to learn what I need to know?

Business. It's all around us—from your telephone company, to the factory that built your car, to that doughnut shop down the street. We all have many dealings with businesses every day. But, despite all of these interactions, business remains something of a mystery to many of us. What exactly do they do all day behind those closed doors? How do you turn a little bit of money into a lot of money? Like that scene in the *Wizard of Oz* when Toto pulls the curtain away to reveal the

LEARNING ABOUT BUSINESS—AND YOURSELF

Today, Joanne Eglash is a successful, Silicon Valley–based consultant and writer. However, before she found success, she knew that she would have to have a plan for achieving it. Not only that, but she knew that she would have to learn some business basics. To accomplish the latter goal, Joanne visited the SBA Web site (www.sba.gov) and obtained free online training. She also interviewed a variety of finance experts to find out more about starting and running a business. The result? Joanne realized that she didn't have to choose between having her own business or working for someone else—she could do *both*.

"Initially, launching my Internet business-to-business consulting company seemed like an all-or-nothing option," says Joanne. "Either I would take a leap of blind faith and rush into consulting full-time, or I would play it safe by remaining an in-house employee working for someone else. I didn't see any alternative." But after learning more about what would be involved in starting and running a business, she realized that she had one more option available to her. "I was able to take a long look at myself and realize I'm the kind of person who wants a certain amount of security. With this insight came self-acceptance. I gave myself permission to keep my day job."

With the security of a regular career to back her up, Joanne started her consulting business and quickly found success. And, as a direct result of her consulting work, she wrote a popular book, *How to Write a .com Business Plan*. As for her advice to other aspiring entrepreneurs, Joanne has this to say: "All of us tend to be anxious about the unknown and hesitate in the face of risk. How you turn that fear into your advantage is what makes you a success."

man operating the machinery who is the "Great and Powerful Oz," many of us may not have a clue what is going on behind the curtain until it is revealed to us.

While most of us have at one time or another worked in a business—and we are certainly familiar with what it's like to be an employee—few of us have ever run a business, much less started one from scratch. So, when it comes time to think about starting a business, it's easy to be overwhelmed by the many different things that we don't understand—what's going on behind the curtain.

The fact is, you don't know what you don't know. The good news is that the mysteries of business can be revealed, and the answers to your questions are all around you.

So, if not knowing anything about starting a business is getting in the way of your dreams of independence, here's what you can do right now. Don't allow the nuts and bolts of business continue to be a mystery—step your way around this obstacle by asking the following questions:

1. What do I *really* need to know to start my business?
2. What *don't* I need to know to start my business?
3. Where are the best places to get the information I need?
4. How can I start with what I've got?

Let's go through these questions in detail. By the time you're done with this chapter, you'll be able to lift the veil of mystery away from starting a business. In addition, you'll understand exactly what you need to know to start your own business, and you'll be able to focus on just that—and not on the things that you don't need to know. You should be well on your way to leaping over this particular barrier and on the path to making your dreams of independence reality.

Question 1: What Do I *Really* Need to Know to Start My Business?

Believe it or not, you don't need to know everything there is to know about business before you start your own business. You don't need a master of business administration (MBA) degree, you don't need to take classes after work at your local community college, and you don't need to buy every book on the business bookshelf at your local bookstore.

When it comes right down to it, there are only a few essentials that you really should know about before you dive into your business. Take a little time to get to know them, and you'll be on your way before you know it. These things include:

learning the nuts and bolts of business,

finding customers, and

keeping track of your money

Remember: There's nothing standing in the way of your starting your own business right now—*this very minute*—except yourself. Think about it. Why aren't you in business right now? What's holding you back? Most successful entrepreneurs don't see barriers; they only see opportunities. To highly motivated entrepreneurs, barriers are simply minor speed bumps on the way to achieving their goals of independence and success. More often than not, they simply blast right through them. And you can, too.

> To highly motivated entrepreneurs, barriers are simply minor speed bumps on the way to achieving their goals of independence and success.

When Barbara Beckstrom and Linda Hicks lost their jobs because the northern Michigan construction firm they worked for went out of business, they soon realized that they just might have been handed a tremendous opportunity to start their own business. Despite the fact that they knew nothing about starting and running their own business, they forged ahead, driven by the excitement of being their own bosses and the need to make money to live. Barbara and Linda started their own company—Right Rail, which specializes in installing highway guardrails and fences. But, rather than allow the fact that they lacked even the most basic knowledge of running a business get in the way of their dreams, they learned all they needed to know about starting and running a business by spending time at their local library, eventually creating a business plan to secure financing to buy equipment and materials and to pay wages. The company quickly grew to annual sales of more than $2 million and eighteen employees.

By deciding you're in business, you *are* in business. That's one of the advantages of free enterprise. You see, in the beginning, it's much more a state of mind than anything else. The formalities of the mechanics of starting your business are details that you can catch up with along the way—just don't wait *too* long to catch up!

Despite this fact, many people allow the mechanics of starting a business (or, more likely, the *fear* of the mechanics) to get in the way of their dreams. Instead of just doing it, they waste days, weeks, and years fretting about the things they don't know, rather than simply diving in and learning along the way as Barbara Beckstrom and Linda Hicks did.

Key Questions: Are you allowing your lack of business knowledge to get in the way of your starting your own business? Do you always seem to have just one more question that needs to be answered, or one more thing to learn, before you can take that last step and open your new business to the world? If so, step back from your questions for a little bit and ask yourself this: "What is the one thing I could do right now to put myself in business?" Here are some suggestions for what that one thing might be:

- *Print business cards with the name of your business, your name and title, and contact information.*
- *Create a flyer announcing your business and deliver copies to all your neighbors.*
- *Send an e-mail message announcing your business to all your friends, relatives, and other acquaintances.*
- *Create a simple, four-page catalog of your products or services on your computer and mail it out to all your friends, relatives, and other acquaintances.*

By doing as few as one of these things—and forgetting all about your other questions, at least for a while—you'll find that your perspective will be changed. Instead of thinking about starting your business, you will be in business.

BUSINESS: ONE BIG GARAGE SALE

Although, from the outside looking in, business may seem to be a mysterious and foreign thing, the basic idea of business is actually quite a simple one: to sell a product or service and make a profit—that is, to have some money left over after you pay your expenses. If you think about it, any business—from the smallest one-person, home-based operation to the largest Fortune 500 corporation—is really nothing more than a great big garage sale.

For starters, every garage sale needs to have products to sell—all the odds and ends that you've been setting aside to sell for months (i.e., the old furniture, clothes, lawnmower, appliances, toys, and other things collecting dust in your garage or home). These many items are just like the products or services that you're going to sell through your own business—they've just seen a bit more use.

> The basic idea of business is actually quite a simple one: to sell a product or service and make a profit—that is, to have some money left over after you pay your expenses.

Of course, every item you sell in your garage sale needs a price. Whether you're selling a stack of old paperback books for 25 cents each or a nice television set for $150, people are going to ask you how much you want for them, and you'll need an answer. Your answer is the price. In a garage sale, you have the option of pricing your items before you start (by sticking price tags on each item) or giving out prices on the fly.

Setting a price is a balancing act between making enough money from the sale to make it worthwhile for you and setting it low enough to attract enough customers to generate the level of sales that you want. Just as it's generally better to have your garage sale prices established in advance (that way there's less chance of confusion as ten people jockey for your attention at the same time), it's also better to have your prices for your new business's products or services established in advance. That way you won't have to fumble around trying to establish the right price when a potential customer asks you how much you charge.

Of course, every successful garage sale needs to attract customers. You can publicize (market) your garage sale in a variety of different ways. For example, you can run an advertisement in the classified ads of a local newspaper or post a notice on a bulletin board in your local grocery store. You can send out an e-mail message to all your nearby family and friends, or you can post signs with directions to your home at key intersections in your neighborhood. Simply having a crowd of eager buyers swarming your driveway is an effective way to attract more people. If you want to turn those you attract into a swarm of buyers, you've got to have the kinds of items that they will find interesting to browse through and buy.

Businesses have to attract the attention of potential customers, too. While they may not do it by posting signs on street corners (there are some exceptions to this rule), they do run advertisements in the media, they do mail out marketing brochures and letters, and they do make personal contact with prospective buyers—and much, much more.

If you sell a lot of things at your garage sale, you'll need to keep track of your money. You might have a shoebox set aside with lots of ones and fives and quarters to make change for your customers and in which you can put the money you receive when you sell an item. Or you might just have a roll of cash stuck in your pocket or purse. In any case, you'll need someplace to keep your garage sale proceeds and to make change for your customers. After your garage sale is over, you'll be able to count your money—deducting the cash you had on hand when you started—to determine how much cash you brought in from your sale.

Regular businesses have to keep track of their money, too, but instead of stashing the cash you bring in from selling your products or services in a pocket, you'll likely put it in a cash register or deposit it into a bank account for safekeeping. Because you're probably going to be handling a lot of money in your business (and having to account to the government for any taxes that your business generates), you'll probably also want to record all your monetary transactions in an accounting software program on your computer.

While most customers at a garage sale will take their purchases along with them, you may offer to deliver particularly large or bulky items to them yourself. Regular businesses deliver products and services, too: on the customer's site (e.g., a house-painting business), through the mail or other delivery service (someone selling handmade birdhouses), or by simply having the customer pick their purchases up at the place of business (e.g., a bakery or coffeehouse).

So, as you can see, the basics of running the business are no more mysterious than having a garage sale one sunny Saturday afternoon. The concepts are all the same. If you can successfully run a garage sale, then there's no reason at all that you can't also run a successful business—it's the same thing. Right? Right!

THE NUTS AND BOLTS OF BUSINESS

While a business is not all that much different from a garage sale, there *are* a few formalities that you'll have to deal with when you decide to start your new business—things you wouldn't have to worry much about if you have the occasional garage sale. These are what we call the "nuts and bolts" of business. Here are some of the aspects of starting a business that you'll need to consider before (or soon after) you begin.

A Name

Every business needs a name, and yours is no different. While most any name will do, you should understand that the name of your business is a marketing tool that can attract clients and customers all by itself. The best business name (1) describes your product or service, (2) is novel, (3) is easily remembered, (4) is easy to spell and pronounce, and (5) is protectable by a trademark or service mark.

When Evelyn Ashley launched her new Atlanta-based law firm, she could have followed the convention of countless attorneys before her and named her firm Ashley & Smith, Attorneys at Law. Instead, to attract attention—and to have a bit of fun—Evelyn Ashley named her new firm The Red Hot Law Group of Ashley. Not only did this name attract tons of attention in the media and among prospective clients, but it also has helped bring Evelyn great success.

Don't forget: It's important that the name of your business does not duplicate the name of another business in your area. Not only can this cause confusion among potential customers, but it can also attract legal attention—something few new business owners can afford to deal with. If, for example, you decided to name your new fast-food restaurant McDonald's, we suspect it wouldn't be long before some big, burly lawyers from Chicago convinced your friendly, local judge to slap you with a restraining order that would force you to drop your name like a hot bag of French fries.

Form of Business

At least seven out of eight small businesses start out as what are known as "sole proprietorships." Why? Because this form of business is the easiest and least expensive to start up, and it requires little or no legal assistance to do so. A *sole proprietorship* simply means that one person owns and operates the business. Any income resulting from the business is taxed as personal income to the sole proprietor.

To become a sole proprietorship, you basically do nothing—no forms to fill out and no permissions to be granted.

You're automatically a sole proprietorship unless you decide to pair up with a friend, relative, or colleague, in which case your business becomes a *partnership*.

Limited liability companies and *corporations* are also options, each of which has unique advantages and disadvantages (particularly in regard to personal liability and taxes), along with increasingly more complex variations and legal requirements (meaning that you're going to have to spend some time and money to get one set up). Our advice is to start with sole proprietorship unless you're advised otherwise by your accountant or attorney for reasons that make sense to you—at least until you get your business up and running and have a chance to see where you want to take it in the future.

Licenses and Permits

Depending on exactly where you live and exactly where you plan to do business, you may be subject to a variety of different legal requirements to be in business. Most cities (and counties as well, if you're not in a city) require owners of businesses to obtain a business license to do business. Depending on where you live, you may also be required to obtain a home occupation permit, a zoning permit, a police permit, a food preparation permit, or any number of other licenses and permits to do business. Check with your local city hall, county government, or chamber of commerce to see what kinds of licenses and permits you'll need to keep your business on the *right* side of the law.

One more thing: If you're going to sell taxable products (and therefore charge customers sales tax), then you'll need a seller's permit or equivalent. These permits are generally issued by your state tax authority.

FINDING CUSTOMERS

Every business needs two things:

Products and services to sell

Customers to buy them

You can have the greatest products and services in the world, but if you don't have customers to buy them, then you're not going to have a business for very long. Finding customers is therefore usually at or near the top of the list of priorities for most new business owners.

Four key approaches to finding customers will help ensure the ongoing health of your business: (1) personal contact, (2) working through others, (3) written communications, and (4) showing what you can do.

Personal Contact

You are your business. As such, you are perhaps its best advertisement and its best salesperson. When you talk to others about your business and your products and services—whether at a church social, or at a chamber of commerce business mixer, or while selling your products at a craft fair—you are marketing and selling. If you're friendly, personable, and honest, people will respond positively, and, if they're interested in buying what you're selling, you're bound to end up increasing your sales as a result.

> You are your business. As such, you are perhaps its best advertisement and its best salesperson.

When Tina Cordova of Albuquerque, New Mexico, decided to quit her job waiting tables at a local Sizzler steakhouse and to start her own construction business—Queston Construction—

along with a business partner, she knew that she would need to get some customers as soon as possible. Sure that the personal touch would work best for her, Tina quickly joined the Albuquerque Hispanic Chamber of Commerce and called every realtor in the organization's directory. Within three days, Tina had her first customers. Tina's company quickly grew from her original crew of three and sales of $50,000 in her first year, to a crew of up to forty people and more than $3 million in annual sales.

Many people have the same dreams as you do—to be their own boss and to find their way to financial independence—and they enjoy talking to someone who is actually making those dreams happen. So long as you're not putting the hard sell on them (few people we know like to be unduly pressured to buy something, regardless of the personality of the person doing the selling), they will carry away a positive message from their interaction with you and may very well become loyal customers and clients.

Some people learn to feel more at ease marketing through personal contact by learning selling and people management skills in training programs as distributors in direct selling organizations. Of course, distributors are in business themselves and thus have the ability to immediately apply what they learn.

Working Through Others

For the vast majority of new and small businesses, referrals—customers that come to you as the result of a personal recommendation from a trusted friend or colleague—are by far the most important source of new business. Not only do they cost you nothing in marketing expenses, but, because they are coming to you as the result of a recommendation from a trusted acquaintance, they are already predisposed to buy from you.

Julie Aigner-Clark started her business, Baby Einstein, when she was unsuccessful in finding age-appropriate products to help

> For the vast majority of new and small businesses, referrals—customers that come to you as the result of a personal recommendation from a trusted friend or colleague—are by far the most important source of new business.

her share her love of art, classical music, language, and poetry with her infant daughter. Using her savings, she created her first Baby Einstein video and then founded her company to market it. In the beginning, Julie relied on "parent-to-parent" word-of-mouth marketing to spread the word about her products. These referrals paid off, with word traveling fast and sales steadily increasing. As her business continued to grow, Julie gradually developed a suite of complementary products including books, discovery cards, and audio CDs. The company was recently acquired by the Walt Disney Company.

So, how can *you* get referrals? You do it by doing great work, by charging a fair price, and by honoring your commitments. The truth is, there are a lot of lousy businesspeople out there—people who sell poor products, who aren't aware of the meaning of the words *customer service,* who are habitually late in delivering their products or performing their services, and who overcharge and underdeliver. Countless customers and clients-to-be are constantly on the lookout for businesses that can do a better job than the lousy ones they are stuck with. Be the best you can be, and you'll get more referrals—and, as a result, more business—than you'll know what to do with.

Written Communications

When you say the word *marketing,* this is what most people think about: advertisements, brochures, Web sites, newsletters, e-mail messages, proposals, flyers, and articles in newspapers and magazines. All are written forms of marketing communications.

Without a doubt, written communications can be very effective—businesses spend millions and millions of dollars every year on advertising campaigns based on written communications. The key for you as a new business owner is to maximize the effectiveness of written marketing communications while minimizing their cost. Advertising in magazines can be very expensive (and it may take several insertions over a period of time to pay off), and, with millions of Web sites already in existence—and more added every day—it's easy for your message to be lost in cyberspace. How are other businesses like yours getting their message out to prospective customers and clients? Which methods work best, and which ones should be avoided?

When Martin and Andrea Swinton decided to try to get the word out about their antique store—Take-a-Boo Emporium in Toronto, Ontario—they took advantage of the local media to get free advertising. They did this by throwing a second anniversary street party, complete with free caricatures for customers and bubble blowing for the children. The event caught the fancy of local media, including newspapers and television, which publicized the event in advance for free.

Before you run off and spend a bunch of money on marketing and sales, take the time to understand the best ways to get your message in front of your *best* customers, and then pursue only those approaches. After every marketing effort, assess how it went to determine whether you should use that particular approach again or try something else.

Showing What You Can Do

For many kinds of businesses, showing what you can do is a particularly effective form of marketing and selling. If you decide to start a gift basket business, for example, imagine how much business you would generate if one of your gift baskets was displayed at a local mall along with your contact information. Or, if you're an architect, think about the potential impact that a beautiful home built to your design along with a sign posted out front with the name of your firm on it will have on your business. When people can see the work that you have done—can experience its quality and see it for themselves—you remove the mystery of what you're going to deliver, while providing a very powerful and attractive incentive for people to buy from you.

Summary

There are many different ways to attract the attention of prospective customers—there is no one best way. The best way is whatever works best for you. Janice Byer of Docu-Type Administrative Services of Caledon East, Ontario, for example, has found that networking is key to her business success. To that end, she joined the Brampton Board of Trade, as well as many online business-related associations. She volunteers as a Web site designer in her community and writes articles for publication in a variety of media, including *Business Woman Canada*, the *RSS Herald*, and About.com.

Key Questions: Finding that first customer is often a stumbling block for many new business owners. To find your way around this barrier ask yourself, "Who do I know who will buy my product or service right now? A friend? A relative? A neighbor? Someone from work?" If the answer is not obvious, how can you get to know people who might buy what you have to sell? Consider the story of Tina Cordova—one of the first things she did to find customers was to join her local Hispanic Chamber of Commerce, where she was able to quickly network with people who were interested in what she had to sell. Is there a similar group in your community that you could join to network in the same way?

KEEPING TRACK OF YOUR MONEY

Why bother keeping track of your money if you have enough revenue to pay all the bills, and if you don't, what good will it do? Isn't it a lot of work—and just one more barrier on your path to starting your own business? Here are a few good reasons for keeping track of your money:

- You'll be able to see how much money is coming *into* your business in sales of products or services.
- You'll be able to see how much money is going *out* of your business in expenses to buy inventory, pay rent, hire employees, fund benefit plans, and cover other costs.
- With these numbers (how much money you brought into and sent out of your business), you'll be able to determine whether you're making a profit—something that's very good to know when you're in business!
- You'll be able to prepare your business taxes quickly and easily. Okay, maybe there's no such thing as "quick and easy" when it comes to taxes, but we guarantee it will be far less painful than if you didn't track your money!

As you can see, there are a number of good reasons for tracking your money. You shouldn't, however, let the fact that you don't know how to keep track of your money stop you from starting your business! The fact is, you'll have plenty of time to learn after you get your business started. Our advice is to just dive in and then worry about sorting out the details later.

The basics of tracking your business's money are actually not all that difficult. If you can add and subtract (and we're sure you can!), then you've pretty much got it nailed. And,

---

FROM THE WRECKAGE, A NEW BUSINESS

When Alexis Demko found herself in high school and pregnant, her dreams of graduating early, going to college, and studying fashion design in Italy were shattered. As a teenage, single mother, Alexis knew that she would have to find a way to support herself and her child—and fast. Her decision: to start her own business. The only problem was, although Alexis had attended a two-week business camp for teenage girls when she was sixteen (Camp Start-UP), she had never started or operated her own business before, and she didn't have a lot of time to learn the ropes. "I told myself," says Alexis, "you don't have to be a loser. You don't have to sit around home all day and wait for somebody to take care of you."

When working for her father's demolition business as a bookkeeper, she had noticed that he routinely threw away a lot of perfectly good items pulled out of the buildings he demolished—items that he had no use for, including cabinets, ceiling tiles, light fixtures, and much more. So Alexis approached her father and asked him whether she could try selling these

---

unless you have a particularly complex business, chances are you can track the money yourself—by using either a good old-fashioned pencil and a piece of paper or, even better, an accounting software package, such as Quicken or Money, or a computer spreadsheet program, such as Excel or Quattro.

When you *are* ready to start tracking your money, here are the basics you should consider:

- *Separate your personal finances from your business finances.* No matter what kind of business you have or what

items instead of his throwing them out. In exchange for giving her the material, her father would receive a percentage of the profits. He agreed, and Demko Demolition Warehouse was born.

Alexis has had to learn on the job, picking up business tips from her father and from others along the way. Alexis's business has been a success, and she was recently named entrepreneur of the month by *CosmoGIRL!* magazine. She has also started taking business and Spanish classes at a local community college—the business classes to learn even more about operating a business effectively, and the Spanish classes to communicate better with her many clients in Mexico (her business is located just outside San Diego, California, near the Mexican border). And she hasn't forgotten her dreams of becoming a fashion designer: She has created a business plan for a manufacturing children's golf clothes and intends to implement it in the not-too-distant future.

form you selected for it, it pays to keep your personal and business finances separate. This means establishing a separate checking account for your business and obtaining (if necessary) a separate charge card. If you don't keep your personal and business finances separate, (1) you'll never have a real sense of whether your business is making money, and (2) you'll have a tough time properly deducting your business expenses for your tax returns.

- *Keep track of all the money you bring into your business.* Whenever you receive a payment for a product or service, note it in your money-tracking system—whether you're using a paper and pencil, a computer spreadsheet, or an accounting software package. Note also who or where it comes from so you'll get an idea of what's working. This money is what drives your business—it pays your bills and eventually becomes your profit.

- *Keep track of all the money you take out of the business.* Every business takes money to set up and operate. The money that you send out of the business to set up and operate it is known as an *expense,* and you'll need to track every expense that your business incurs. Typical business expenses include rent, utilities, payroll, insurance, the cost of materials and inventory, Internet access, business travel, telephone, office supplies, and much, much more.

- *Keep track of the difference between the money you bring into your business and the money you take out of your business.* When you subtract your expenses from your revenues (the money you bring into your business), the number you have left over is your *profit.* If the number is negative (meaning that your expenses exceed your revenue), then you've got a loss instead of a profit. Most businesses are in a loss position when they first start up, eventually moving into the profit column once they begin to take off.

These basics are really all you need to get your business off the ground and running and will be more than sufficient to keep you organized and on track. As your business grows, you'll eventually need to set up a more formal system to deal with your increasingly complex transactions. But why worry about that now? The most important thing is for you to go ahead and get your business started; otherwise, you won't have any money to keep track of at all!

Question 2: What *Don't* I Need to Know to Start My Business?

As we pointed out earlier in this chapter, there is a lot of business knowledge out there. In fact, there is so much information that it's easy to be overwhelmed worrying whether you should find out one more thing before you get your business off the ground. However, if you decide to hold off on your plans to start your own business until you have investigated, digested, and understood all there is to know, you'll *never* get your business off the ground.

The fact is, there are some kinds of business knowledge that you should definitely have at least a passing acquaintance with—either before or shortly after you start your business (see question 1)—and there are some kinds of business knowledge that you really don't have to learn to start your business. Once your business is off the ground and starts to grow, you can turn your attention to these latter topics as necessary.

So, rather than getting tangled up in one more roadblock on your path to success, avoid diving into these business topics until your business is well under way, if they are necessary at all:

Strategic planning

Organizational behavior

Leadership

Management

Knowledge management

Human resources

A GREAT BUSINESS IDEA IS BORN

While working as a designer's assistant, Liz Lange's pregnant friends kept asking her whether she could help them find fashionable maternity wear. The problem was, the vast majority of maternity wear was stuck in a kind of fashion black hole—lots of oversized dresses and pants, with cutouts and large, expandable Lycra panels. When she looked into it, Liz quickly realized that there was nothing out there for the woman who wanted to look as good pregnant as she did before she became pregnant. "I was almost offended by what was being offered for pregnant women," she says. "[Nine months] is a fairly long period of time, and women are just too active today. It's too much a part of life to have to sit out nine months wearing a big tent, not feeling good about themselves." Despite the fact that she knew nothing about starting and running a business, Liz vowed that she would do something about it. And that's exactly what she did. She kicked off her business by designing a few pieces that combined fashion and function—with the emphasis on fashion.

Financial analysis

Economics

And pretty much anything not covered in question 1

Key Questions: Are you delaying starting your new business because you want to learn everything there is to know about business first? Are you letting your lack of business knowledge get in the way of your dreams of independence? Remember: Some of the most successful entrepreneurs didn't know anything about business when they started their own companies. But, while they didn't have a formal business edu-

Excited about her designs, Liz took them to retailers and gave them her pitch. But, instead of jumping on the bandwagon, retailers were decidedly skeptical about the prospects for such a product. Says Liz, "They told me, 'Pregnant women will not spend money. It's a category that we have no interest in. If you want to go ahead, be prepared to do it on your own because we won't be selling any maternity clothing.'" Convinced that she could turn her idea into a successful enterprise, Liz forged ahead, borrowing start-up funding from family and friends, and opening an office in New York City. Soon, women began to spread the word about Liz's unique take on maternity wear, and business began to boom. Then, a *New York Times* article put her business on the map in a big way, pushing her to move into a larger location in Manhattan and to open stores in Long Island and Beverly Hills. Liz's business continues to grow; sales are now more than $3 million a year.

cation, they were determined to be successful, and they didn't let anything stand in the way of achieving their goals. They found—as you will when you get your business started—that there is plenty of time to learn on the job.

Question 3: Where Are the Best Places to Get the Information I Need?

It's easy—and perfectly normal—to feel overwhelmed when presented with the challenge of starting your own business. Where do you start? What kinds of licenses are required? Will your community zoning laws allow you to run your business out of your home? Will you have to charge sales tax, and, if so, what do you do with it? Do you need to hire an accountant? Should you accept credit cards, and, if so, how do you set up a merchant's account? What do you have to do to find a wholesaler?

There are thousands of potential questions that you can ask, and there are just as many potential sources of answers to your questions for you to explore. The secret is first to find high-quality, reliable sources of information that aren't just infomercials for some expensive get-rich-quick money-making system and to get your information in the ways that you enjoy most. Do you prefer to read (books, magazines, Web sites), listen (tapes, CDs), watch (videos, live seminars, DVDs), or talk (chat rooms, one-on-one meetings, teleclasses)? Whichever your preference, be sure to use the sources that are most effective for you.

> It's important to learn enough to get your business off the ground, but not to get so deep into your research that you become paralyzed by it.

Keep one thing in mind: It's important to learn enough to get your business off the ground, but not to get so deep into your research that you become paralyzed by it. It's easy to become overwhelmed by the amount of information available on the subject of starting your own business. It's the old "paralysis by analysis" syndrome—a formidable roadblock to success if you're not careful.

BOOKS

Many, many books are available on selecting, starting, and running your own business. While some take you through the entire process, others focus on particular areas, and you should choose the books you will buy and read based on your own specific needs. For example, if you need to know more about tracking your money, choose a book that focuses on that topic. If, on the other hand, you're not sure exactly what legal requirements you'll need to meet to start your business, then choose a book that covers that aspect in detail. And, if you need it all, then choose a book that covers everything about selecting, starting, and running your business.

Here are some of our books that can help you with basic business knowledge but are different from the material in this book:

- *Finding Your Perfect Work* (Tarcher, 2003). Best for people willing to do personal exploration and read about what actual people have done in hundreds of examples. It includes appendices with a survey for determining your personal style matchable with a directory of over 1,500 self-employment careers.
- *The Best Home Businesses for the 21st Century* (Tarcher, 1999). Complete profiles on ninety-five top businesses, complete with detailed information on necessary knowledge and skills, start-up costs, advantages, disadvantages, potential earnings, first steps, and much, much more.
- *Home-Based Business for Dummies*, with Peter Economy (Wiley, 2001). A complete guide to selecting, starting, and running your business, particularly geared to people who wish to start a business in their homes.
- *Working from Home* (Tarcher, 1999). Covers pricing; taxes; insurance; legal and zoning matters; juggling family, friends, and children; and much more.

Of course, lots of other books are available—by all sorts of authors—and you should take time to browse through them at your local bookstore or at an online bookstore such as

Amazon.com or Barnes & Noble online (www.bn.com). See which books best answer the questions you have and best fit your own personality. And be sure to ask anyone you know who has successfully started a business what books, if any, proved to be of value.

LIBRARIES

Libraries are another great place to spend some time. Not only do libraries often stock a pretty good selection of books addressing basic business knowledge, but they also generally carry a vast selection of magazines that cover the topic as well. *Inc.*, *Entrepreneur*, *Home Business*, *Fast Company*, and many others can often be found at your nearby local library. And if it doesn't carry the magazine you're looking for, ask the staff there to subscribe!

Another good reason to spend some time at your local library is free (or inexpensive) access to the Internet if you do not have your own access to the Web. This can be a real lifesaver until such time as you can afford to buy a computer and sign up with an Internet service provider. Libraries also offer rather expensive directories and other reference materials—such as the Foundation Center's *FC-Search* and the Gale *Directories in Print*—that you would never consider buying on your own. You will usually find directories at the library reference desk, which is staffed by a librarian who can help you find resources you may not otherwise encounter.

> Another good reason to spend some time at your local library is free (or inexpensive) access to the Internet if you do not have your own access to the Web.

WEB SITES

Web sites are some of the very best places to go to get information on basic business knowledge, much of it for free. Many of the magazines listed earlier have their own Web sites chock-full of information—taken from both the printed editions of the magazines as well as special resources (including bulletin boards, chat rooms, articles, links to other Web sites, etc.) that are available only there. Here are some of our favorite Web sites for business knowledge:

AOL's Small Business Channel: www.aol.com

CCH Business Owner's Toolkit: www.toolkit.cch.com

Entrepreneur.com: www.entrepreneur.com

Small Business Administration: www.sba.gov

ChamberBiz: www.chamberbiz.com

Startup Journal *(Wall Street Journal)*: www.startupjournal.com

EntreWorld: www.entreworld.org

Edward Lowe PeerSpectives: www.peerspectives.org

U.S. Business Advisor: www.business.gov

Business.com: www.business.com

One thing to keep in mind about Web sites is that there is a public Web (free sites, including search engines such as Google [www.google.com] and many of the sites listed here) and a private Web (pay sites). When you're in the early stages of researching basic business knowledge, it's definitely in your interest to stick with the public Web as much as possible. There is an overwhelming amount of free information out there on starting and running a business, and therefore little reason to pay for it.

Once you choose your business and get it started, you may then find it advantageous to join a pay site that provides you with the information you need to find highly specific information of value to you. For using the private Web, you may get better results at less cost using the services of an information professional. You can locate one at www.aiip.org, the site of the professional association for this field.

EXISTING BUSINESS OWNERS

Existing business owners can potentially be your very best source of general business knowledge. Why? Because they have been there, done that—perhaps many times over. And, while they may have many lessons of success to teach you, they will surely also have many lessons of failure—lessons that you should learn from, too, so you'll avoid making the same mistakes.

> By far, the vast majority of successful business owners simply love to talk about their businesses, and they are generally more than happy to talk with someone who is thinking of starting a business.

Chances are, you probably already know someone who has his or her own business— a friend, a relative, a neighbor, a work associate, the owner of a local business that you frequent. If you're worried that a successful entrepreneur won't want to give you the time of day, don't be. By far, the vast majority of successful business owners simply love to talk about their businesses, and they are generally more than happy to talk with someone who is thinking of starting a business.

If you don't know someone, then check out the bulletin boards or chat rooms located at some of the Web sites that cater to people starting up their own businesses. iVillage.com (www.ivillage.com), for example, has many, very active boards—full of successful small-business people who love to give advice to those who aren't sure what kind of business they want to start or what first steps to take. While they're not going to make the money for you, they will do their best to get you to the point where you can start making money yourself. Give it a try!

One more thing: You can also learn a lot from *retired* business owners. SCORE, the Service Corps of Retired Executives, is available in most medium to large U.S. cities to help anyone interested in starting their own business. When Beth Flanders decided to start her Rhode Island–based laser printing and document management business—Document Technologies— she first approached her local SCORE office for advice, where she received assistance on creating business, marketing, and financial plans. Armed with these plans, Beth was able to quickly land an SBA-guaranteed loan from a local bank, putting her business on the map in a big way.

TRADE OR PROFESSIONAL ASSOCIATIONS

It seems that just about every conceivable profession has a trade or professional association that represents its members. Canadian writers who write articles and books on science topics have the Canadian Science Writers Association (www.interlog .com/~cswa/); quilters have the National Quilting Association (www.nqaquilts.org); bookkeepers have the American Institute of Professional Bookkeepers (www.aipb.com); medical billing specialists have the Healthcare Billing and Management Association (www.hbma.com); pet sitters have the National Association of Registered Petsitters (www.dogsit.com)—the list goes on and on.

So, what can associations do for you? Here are just a few of the benefits of joining an association or utilizing its resources:

- Associations often provide listings of members, giving you a resource for contacting other people with the same work interests as you and an easy way to advertise your own services to the outside world once you join.

- Associations often provide continuing education to its members, as well as articles on industry trends and news about the field. Articles are often available for free on association Web sites (thus providing a great avenue for your own research efforts) or via member magazines or newsletters.

- Local association chapters often have regular meetings (monthly, every other month, quarterly) where members are able to exchange information, hear guest speakers, network, and stay up-to-date with current events in their field. Chapters often welcome prospective members to attend these meetings, providing you with a great opportunity to meet successful people doing the work you would like to do and to ask them questions or make arrangements to meet with them later.

- Many associations offer test-based certification programs that ensure your knowledge is up to par in your chosen field, while providing your clients (and clients-to-be) with the peace of mind of knowing that you are a highly skilled professional.

- Many associations sponsor national conventions where you'll have the opportunity to network with people from across the country, participate in numerous educational opportunities, and enter your work (depending on the kind of work you do) in judged shows or competitions. An added benefit: These conventions are often held in some very nice places to visit (San Diego, New York City, New

---

SURVEY SAYS . . .

In a survey of one hundred business owners, *Small Business Success* magazine collected the following information about key aspects of starting and running a successful business:

- The key to business success is business knowledge.
- Word of mouth is most important for small-business marketing success.
- The best competitive advantage is experience.
- Customer awareness is essential to marketing.
- The largest potential trouble spot is too-fast growth.

Orleans, Denver, Chicago, etc.), and the expense of attending them may be tax-deductible.

EDUCATIONAL OPPORTUNITIES

Every community has a number of educational opportunities for learning basic business knowledge; the larger your community, the more opportunities you'll find. Even if your community doesn't have the exact opportunities to meet your specific needs, there are also many remote opportunities available through the mail or via the Internet. Here are just a few of the possibilities:

Community colleges

Four-year college and university programs

Graduate schools of business (for an MBA)

Distance learning programs

University extension programs

Internet-based (online) learning programs

> **Key Questions:** *Did you already know about these information resources? If so, have you explored them fully? If not, ask yourself, "What's been keeping me from pursuing them?" If that's where you're stuck, don't think results at this point; think curiosity. What would happen if you spent some time in the library doing research on your business? Or made appointments to meet with several successful business owners and discuss the lessons they learned along the way? And so on. What might you discover that could lead you to the answer you've been missing?*

PLOWING AWAY OBSTACLES

To fill the gaps in her seasonal ice and snow removal business, Celeste Gleave of Layton, Utah, decided to start a new business: selling advertising as an independent contractor for a Utah-based publishing company. When the company suddenly closed its doors over the President's Day weekend, she and her many customers who had paid money for very expensive advertisements to be run in *Utah Preservation* magazine (which had not yet been published) were left high and dry. Instead of telling her customers that their money was gone, Celeste took out a second mortgage on her house and borrowed money to buy all the equipment necessary to publish her own magazine: computers, scanners, and specialized publishing software. There was only one problem: Celeste didn't know anything at all about publishing and marketing a magazine,

Question 4: How Can I Start with What I've Got?

Now comes a moment of truth. You have acquired some level of business knowledge. While you also know that there's more you could know, you want to get under way and start producing some income. Do you know enough to start?

For most businesses, we believe that if you know enough to get started, then you're ready to go. Here's why: You learn as you go. Chances are your business may take a turn you didn't expect, as Sylvie Charrier's did in chapter 2. It's not unusual for the customers you land to want something different than what you expected. For example, you may find that customers want maintenance services instead of products.

and she definitely didn't know anything about using all the computer hardware and software she had just bought. As she says, "I was used to a PC, but all the graphics people were working on Macintoshes, so that's what I bought. The two platforms are completely different. I knew how to work on a PC. I had to call someone to tell me how to turn the Mac on!"

But, rather than allow these formidable obstacles to get in her way, she was determined to make her dream a reality. Over a four-month period, Celeste taught herself how to use the complex graphics software she had purchased (*and* how to turn on her Mac!), and she completed her magazine. She did such a great job that the state of Utah granted her company—FYVE*STAR, Inc.—a five-year contract to produce *Utah Preservation*.

Maybe you do need more time to get just a bit more information or do more research before you announce the opening of your business. If you truly don't feel ready to start, check out more of the ways to acquire know-how that we've shared under the prior question about the best places to get information. However, we have found some people use a lack of business knowledge as an excuse for not going forward.

Maybe the simple fact is that you can't start as big as you'd like or you'll have to keep your day job and start out small-time on the side (not a bad idea, as far as we're concerned). Maybe you'll need to take temp work or a part-time job while you get things going.

Wherever you find yourself, you are not stuck unless you choose to be. Simply doing whatever it is you need to do next will get you past the information obstacle that's been hanging you up.

So, at this point, ask yourself:

What can I do now?

Not what do you *wish* you could do. Or what you *hope* to do. But what you actually *can* do now. Then do it. And keep moving ahead based on what you discover. Refuse to let what seems like a lack of business knowledge become a lifelong obstacle. Millions of people have gotten past this obstacle by doing whatever it is they can do right now. And so can you! Just keep asking . . .

What can I do now?

Our Bias

Regarding the things you need to know to start a business, we have to admit that we have a bias. We believe in doing your homework. To do it well will take months but not years. When you can answer the three questions that follow, chances are you'll learn more by acting rather than waiting. You'll learn other things you need to know about the business as you run it. Celeste Gleave didn't wait until she knew everything she needed to know about publishing before she started her business—she simply dove in, buying the equipment and software she needed and then learning how to use it on the fly.

So, are you ready to dive in? Here are the three final questions to ask yourself as you get ready to jump:

1. *Have you decided what kind of business you would like to start?* Is it possible that the reason you're still dragging your feet is because you still aren't sure exactly what kind of business it is that you'd like? If you're not absolutely sure about what it is that you want to do, then turn to chapter 2 and work your way through the exercises and questions contained therein. Once you decide exactly what business it is that you want to start, come back to this chapter to see exactly what kinds of business knowledge you'll need to get it off the ground.

2. *What do you need to know to start your business?* As we've seen in this chapter, there are only a few things that you need to know about business and many other things that you can ignore—at least until your business starts to grow. And, while each business is different, requiring unique sets of knowledge to operate, there are certain basics that every business owner should quickly learn. These basics include (1) the nuts and bolts described earlier, (2) finding customers, and (3) keeping track of your money. Figure these things out, and you'll be able to take your business pretty far before you have to worry about anything else.

3. *How can you get the information you still lack as quickly as possible?* Once you've figured out exactly what you

need to know about business to get your company started, the next step is to figure out how to get this information as quickly as possible. It's easy to get caught up in paralysis by analysis—continuing to put off starting your business as you decide to learn more about something that really won't have a direct impact on your immediate success. Some sources of the information you need are better (and quicker) than others. One of the best (and fastest) is to talk with people who have successfully started the same kind of business that you would like to run. You may be surprised to hear this, but many business owners are more than happy to spend time telling their story to others who would like to open businesses like theirs—including all the successes and failures along the way. What better way to learn what you need to know about starting a business?

Now from the issues and information in this chapter, identify three things you want or need to do. Write them down in the Personal Action Plan in Appendix A: Take-Off Section, beginning on page 294.

CHAPTER SIX

All Talk, No Action: Is It Me? Do I Have Hang-Ups! Part I

Why can't I leave this job even though I hate it?

I'm just too afraid that I'll fail.

What if I haven't picked the right business?

There's always something to keep me from getting started.

I'm just too overwhelmed/depressed/anxious/busy.

Okay, you've thought about it, talked about it, read about it, and probably even taken some steps to become your own boss, but despite all you've done, all you've learned, and all the information you've gathered, you're still at your job. You're no closer to actually being your own boss. What's wrong? If you're beginning to wonder whether it's a personal hang-up or something about you, you're one step ahead.

Most people who have a personal hang-up about becoming their own boss don't admit it. It's not them. It's the money. It's the economy. It's their family. It's not the right time. Or they need more time. Something else always prevents them from getting on with going out on their own. It's easy to rationalize why you can't go ahead with your plans.

It's like deciding to have a baby. There never seems to be enough money, and it's never just the right time. And, to top it off, the economy is always a reliable scapegoat because it's always in flux. But we're sure you've noticed that some people do defy these ubiquitous impediments and get started anyway. So, if you can't seem to move forward even though you have the information you need and a good plan, and you still really want to be your own boss, then it's time to take a look at yourself.

Like the batter who's in a slump or the writer who's blocked, *you* could be the cause of your crisis in confidence. But don't freak out. Getting snagged on a personal hang-up isn't a reason to despair or get down on yourself. You're not defective. There's nothing wrong with you. Personal hang-ups are out of your awareness. Your hang-ups are like a default setting on your computer. Sometime in the past, you programmed it into your brain for what was probably a good reason at the time and then forgot about it. Since then, it's been working away doing its job without any attention from you.

We all have countless such automatic settings in our brains, but now, in this circumstance, one or more particular default settings are not working for you. And just as you would with the settings on your computer, you need to locate the forgotten defaults, select the new settings you need, and reset them.

To free yourself from whatever's hanging you up and get on with implementing your plans, take a stab at the following questions:

1. What default settings are hanging me up?
2. What new settings do I need?
3. How do I reset my settings?

Question 1: What Default Settings Are Hanging Me Up?

Fear of success. Fear of failure. Fear of rejection. Fear of not being good enough. On and on. There are many labels for our hang-ups. But too often they sound more like an indictment than a cure. To get on with your life, you don't need labels; you need to find the specific mental default settings that are hanging you up. You've unintentionally put an automatic hold on some of the abilities you need to go out on your own. What are they? When did you put them on hold and why? And does this hold still have anything useful to contribute to your situation now?

To answer these questions, let's take a look at the type of reactions you're having to your situation right now. They are symptoms that can point you to the outdated and dysfunctional mental settings that are keeping you from taking the actions you need to take. Here are seven capabilities that are essential to starting a business. Check any of the items listed that apply to your life, particularly to your thoughts and feelings about starting a business. Add up the number of items you've checked for each capability in the spaces provided.

> To get on with your life, you don't need labels; you need to find the specific mental default settings that are hanging you up.

A STORY OF HANG-UPS

At first when Carolyn decided to start her own consulting firm, she was excited and eager. She was underpaid and underappreciated as the manager of a nursing care facility. Her colleagues at other facilities would frequently tell her, "You should leave this place. I'll be your first client."

With their encouragement, she decided to set up a home office, do some financial projections, and talk specifics with several possible clients. Every step was a green light. It appeared she could easily match her measly salary and possibly double her income within a year. In her enthusiasm, she even designed a business card and stationery. As she did these things, her energy level rose dramatically. She seemed to come alive, freed from some of the malaise of years trapped in a dead-end job.

But when the time came to give notice to her employer, Carolyn froze. She couldn't be sure her plans would work. She was a widow of ten years with two daughters to support. What if things didn't go according to plan? What if she wasn't able to earn what she was making now? What if . . . ? She decided now wasn't the best time to make such a change. Her girls would be going to a new junior high school in a month. It would be too traumatic for them if she changed everything now. She'd wait until after school started. September came and went, and she realized that the

Capability 1—Seizing Opportunities

Thinking on Your Own

- ❏ Frequently worried, concerned, and fearful of the unknown

- ❏ Fraught with "what if" scenarios and doubts

holidays would be coming up soon. It still wasn't the right time. Besides, the computer she had at home kept breaking down. She really needed to wait until she could afford to buy a new one.

But as the holidays neared, Carolyn fumed over how little money she had for holiday festivities and gifts, swearing that she'd give notice after the first of the year. But then her daughter decided to compete in the spring pep squad tryouts, and Carolyn's father, divorced and living alone upstate, needed her to take a week off to come care for him after he had surgery. She couldn't take time off for situations like this if she was starting a business, and, besides, she could hardly keep up with all the things she had to do as it was.

And so it was that a year passed since Carolyn had printed her business cards. They spilled out of a drawer while she was cleaning one day, and she sat down on the floor and cried. She had come face-to-face with herself. It wasn't her kids. It wasn't her father. It was her own fear that was keeping her stuck. "I wish I was like my brother," she lamented. "He's fearless. He's been out on his own for years. But I don't seem to have what it takes."

❏ Nagging feeling that something bad is going to happen
❏ Replaying a history of failures

Making Effective Decisions
❏ Lots of undone projects
❏ Bogged down in analysis paralysis and confusion

❏ Suffering from information overload

❏ Difficulty planning and managing your time

❏ Feeling mentally conflicted and nervous

Total Number of Items Checked: ____ of 9

Capability 2—Focusing

Discovering Where You Fit

❏ Disorganized

❏ Unable to make clear decisions

❏ Can't seem to communicate clearly

❏ Difficulty concentrating

Doing What Needs to Be Done

❏ Wanting to have things go your way and be in control all the time

❏ Having trouble controlling your expenses

❏ Worrying about how to keep everything together

❏ Feeling like your life is controlled by others and your situation

Total Number of Items Checked: ____ of 8

Capability 3—Holding Your Own

Taking Action on Your Behalf

❏ Easy to anger, tendency to fly off the handle or frequently curse

❏ Feeling hostile and angry about your current situation

❏ Impatient

❏ Indecisive

Speaking Out for Yourself

- ❏ Anxious, fearful about the future
- ❏ Forgetful
- ❏ Burned out, chronically tired, or having difficulty handling high-pressure situations
- ❏ Unable to sleep

Staying Ahead of the Curve

- ❏ Tired of same old routine
- ❏ Feeling stifled
- ❏ Needing room to breathe
- ❏ Can't catch up

Total Number of Items Checked: _____ of 12

Capability 4—Taking Care of Business

Commanding Respect

- ❏ Feeling bored
- ❏ Tired of self-sacrificing
- ❏ Lack of self-confidence
- ❏ Difficulty setting boundaries and saying no
- ❏ Wishing you were more like someone else

Releasing Your Brakes

- ❏ Others seem to have what you deserve
- ❏ Others get the credit for what you've done
- ❏ Feeling resentful of others' success
- ❏ Feeling unrewarded

Attracting Success Without Distress

- ❏ Uncomfortable with change

- ❏ Overly sensitive to criticism

- ❏ Taking things personally

- ❏ Fear of selling

- ❏ Entangled in problems from the past or from handling the problems of others

Protecting Your Assets

- ❏ Overreacting to things

- ❏ Not feeling safe or trusting you'll be able to protect yourself

- ❏ Pushing yourself too hard or having frequent illnesses

- ❏ Giving up easily

- ❏ Worrying you're not worthy or won't get enough business

Total Number of Items Checked: _____ of 19

Capability 5—Going for What You Want

Being Appreciated for Who You Are

- ❏ Feeling irritable or bitchy, complaining

- ❏ Feeling or fearing rejection

- ❏ Always trying to please others, sometimes resenting it

Taking Problems in Stride

- ❏ Having trouble motivating yourself

- ❏ Feeling you're under a lot of stress

❏ Taking problems so seriously that there's little time for joy

❏ Can't stand up to criticism or attacks from others

Being Up to the Challenge

❏ Feeling tired, de-energized, listless, hopeless

❏ Others are draining your energy

❏ Unwilling to talk about problems or difficulties

❏ Drinking lots of coffee

Turning What You've Got into What You Want

❏ Moping around, feeling sad and depressed

❏ Hate to be alone

❏ Constantly feeling hungry

❏ Lots of complaining

Handling Whatever Comes Along

❏ Bogged down in details or difficulty understanding new things

❏ Worrying about money

❏ Your work isn't as high-quality as expected or as you'd like

❏ Pretending everything is fine

❏ Finding it hard to take your situation

Total Number of Items Checked: _____ of 20

Capability 6—Giving Your Best

Having What It Takes

- ❏ Difficulty collecting money you're owed
- ❏ Self-doubt
- ❏ Suffering from a recent loss
- ❏ Believe you'll lose at whatever you try

Remaining Both Excited and Realistic

- ❏ Addictions to alcohol, drugs, cigarettes
- ❏ Crying and sobbing a lot
- ❏ Easily excitable

Confronting Your Fears

- ❏ Avoiding confrontations or uncomfortable situations
- ❏ Unexplained fears
- ❏ Feeling shy and withdrawn
- ❏ Feel nauseous when under pressure

Creating with Others

- ❏ Feeling apathetic
- ❏ Need to do things yourself
- ❏ Feeling alone or isolated

Total Number of Items Checked: _____of 14

Capability 7—The Strength to Make It

Keeping the Thorns Out of Your Side

- ❏ Putting up and shutting up instead of speaking out about what bothers you

❏ Feeling overburdened

❏ Refusing to talk about your problems

❏ Seems there's always something getting in the way of your doing what you want

Achieving Success and Avoiding Failure

❏ Keep getting into hassles, hold grudges, and/or have ongoing feuds

❏ Blame others for your problems

❏ Hate your current situation, but continue to endure it

❏ Feeling irritable, angry, and annoyed

❏ Equipment continually breaking down or won't work

Total Number of Items Checked: ____of 9

Overview of Totals

Capability 1—Seizing Opportunities: ____ of 9

Capability 2—Focusing: ____ of 8

Capability 3—Holding Your Own: ____ of 12

Capability 4—Taking Care of Business: ____ of 19

Capability 5—Going for What You Want: ____ of 20

Capability 6—Giving Your Best: ____ of 14

Capability 7—The Strength to Make It: ____ of 9

Question 2: What New Settings Do I Need?

Take a look at the capabilities for which you checked the most issues. These are the areas where you're hung up.

CAROLYN'S SCORES

Here are Carolyn's scores and how they relate to her story:

Capability 1—Seizing Opportunities: 2 of 9

Capability 2—Focusing: 2 of 8

Capability 3—Holding Your Own: 6 of 12

Capability 4—Taking Care of Business: 6 of 19

Capability 5—Going for What You Want: 10 of 20

Capability 6—Giving Your Best: 3 of 14

Capability 7—The Strength to Make It: 8 of 9

Carolyn could see she was primarily getting hung up in three areas:

7—The Strength to Make It

3—Holding Your Own

5—Going for What You Want

You can see hints of these hang-ups in her story:

Capability 7: She hated her miserable job situation, yet she had put up with it for years without protest. She was feeling overburdened by her responsibilities but put a positive spin on them. There always seemed to be something in the way of starting up her management company. She blamed her daughters and her father, the equipment breakdowns, the holidays, and so forth.

Capability 3: Being a widow with two young daughters, Carolyn felt her life was controlled by her situation. She worried about being able to hold everything together and meeting all her responsibilities. Yet she was growing increasingly tired of the same old routine and felt stifled on her job. When she didn't have the money she needed, she felt irritated and angry about her situation, especially since she could hardly keep up with things as they were.

Capability 5: Carolyn couldn't motivate herself to do what she wanted to do because of her focus on pleasing everyone but herself: her boss, her daughters, her father. Her focus on others' needs and problems was draining her energy. She was bogged down in the details of their lives and took her responsibilities so seriously that there was little time for her to relax and enjoy herself. That left her feeling tired and de-energized. Despite how hard her situation was to take, she pretended everything was fine and didn't talk to anyone about her difficulties.

Her situation had gone on for so long after she decided to start her company that when the business cards she'd had printed fell from the drawer a year later, she collapsed into feelings of hopelessness.

You can undoubtedly see how these hang-ups reinforced and supported one another. By focusing on the needs of others, Carolyn couldn't go for what she wanted. Ironically, keeping up a strong front while not taking care of her own needs sapped her energy, leaving her without the strength to change her situation.

As human beings, we're born with these seven capabilities. They're innate, inborn, part of our biology. Actually, they are survival skills or instincts. You've undoubtedly used them effectively at other times in your life or found ways to avoid having them without endangering your well-being. In fact, if at some time you decided to put a hold on any of them, it was most likely because, given your circumstances, it wasn't safe for you to use these capabilities. But now, to go out on your own, you need them, and your mind still has them on automatic hold.

Why would you have put these vital capabilities on hold? And what new settings do you need to make so they'll kick in for you again when you need them? *You can discover the answers by reviewing the discussions here of the particular capabilities where the reactions you checked earlier suggest you've got hang-ups.* For each of the seven capabilities, you'll find an explanation of the most common reasons for turning them off, a list of Warning Signals, Reset Suggestions, and an RX Summary for avoiding future hang-ups.

CAPABILITY 1 — SEIZING OPPORTUNITIES

Starting a business requires figuring out clearly what you want to do so you can plan, make effective decisions, and avoid problems. If you've put an automatic hold on your ability to think for yourself and make your own decisions, your efforts to go out on your own will get hung up no matter how much you want to proceed or how much information you have. You need to be able to sort through the information you've

> Starting a business requires figuring out clearly what you want to do so you can plan, make effective decisions, and avoid problems.

gathered, analyze the complexities and unknowns involved in going out on your own, and make decisions with clarity and confidence.

Instead, if you're having difficulty here, you're playing mind games with yourself, worrying about repeating mistakes from the past or letting fears and "what if" worries about what might happen stop you. Why would you do that? Why would you turn off your ability to make sense out of your situation and see the possibilities that are open to you? Here are some common reasons we all can do that at times.

Deciding to go out on your own is replete with unknowns. Everything is an experiment, and nothing is guaranteed. Because most of us have little preparation for being our own boss, we're flooded with new information and invariably run into unexpected complications. So, if you're a person who thinks you must understand and control everything, the decision to become your own boss may send you into a tizzy.

Or, if as a child or in your previous employment, you were never encouraged or were even discouraged to think clearly on your own, make your own decisions, and then act on them, suddenly being in the position to do so can be quite disorienting. Of course, if there's any part of you that isn't so sure you're doing the right thing by going out on your own, shutting down or slowing down your ability to think through and understand your business options is one way to make sure you won't proceed.

Whatever reasons led you to shut down your abilities to seize opportunities, the solution is to reset your mental computer to think about your situation in the here and now. Don't let your mind run away with "what if's" about what might happen or negative past scenarios. Worrying and feeling pressured are not normal or helpful states of mind. Complication and confusion are not necessary. They can make you nervous and ultimately cause you to give up on your goals. So don't overload your mental computer. That's how you turn off your ability to understand what you need to do.

Warning Signals

When you hear yourself say (or feel like saying) any of the following, you're on overload, and you've slipped into a dysfunctional default position:

"I can't decide."

"I don't know what to do."

"I can't handle all this."

"But what if . . . ?"

"I don't see any (other) options."

"This is too complicated."

"I can't keep it all straight."

"I just don't get it."

Reset Suggestions

Whenever you hear these signals, you need to stop! *Stop* thinking about whatever you're thinking about. Bring your attention into the here and now. Notice what you're feeling. When you're in your head, you can't know what you're feeling, and your feelings can run away with you. Shift your attention away from what you don't know to what you do know. Turn your attention away from what's upsetting you to what will help make sense

> Don't overload your mental computer. That's how you turn off your ability to understand what you need to do.

of your current situation. Switch your worry, fear, or anxiety into curiosity by asking, "How can I make sense of this?" or "What does make sense here?" Then put your brain to work breaking down whatever issues, information, or activities you're dealing with into small pieces that you can understand.

If you find yourself slipping often into the old "Don't think" default position, working with a coach or counselor can help you sort out all the feelings, complications, and demands involved in starting a business.

RX Summary

Thinking on Your Own
- Approach problems and concerns with curiosity instead of worry.
- Use curiosity to figure out possibilities and experience "Ah-ha's."
- Stop worrying about what might happen or could happen, and focus on what you want to have happen.
- When concerned, ask, "What's the worst thing that could happen? How could I handle that?"
- When stumped, ask, "What would I do if I knew what to do?"

Making Effective Decisions
- Take the time to digest, process, and segment the information you have.
- Sort out and organize your thoughts, ideas, and feelings.
- Talk or write out the issues to clarify your thoughts and feelings.
- Make your own decisions based on your evaluations and conclusions.
- Take long walks.

CAPABILITY 2 — FOCUSING

Much of business success rests on being in the right place at the right time, doing the right thing. Although that may seem like a matter of chance, it's not. It's a matter of being able to see the big picture and then to zero in on how what you want to do fits into the whole. This enables you to decide what's important so you can drop the unimportant things from your life and organize your time, energy, and resources around what will work. That's what focusing is all about.

Going out on your own requires not only that you focus on your business itself in terms of what you're offering and to whom but also that you sort through all the possible demands on your time, money, and energy, prioritizing them so you can focus your attention on what's most important to achieve your goals within the context of your circumstances. Although such focus is one of the most important prerequisites for starting a successful business, it remains the most pervasive hang-up people encounter in trying to get under way.

If this is where you're hung up, chances are you're trying to do it all and to be all things to all people. As a result, you're becoming scattered and overcommitted. You're getting behind and overwhelmed. Things are starting to feel like they're beyond your control, and you're having trouble following through on your plans. Prospective clients and customers may also be getting confused about who you are and what you're offering. Thus, you may not be getting the kind of reactions from them you're expecting or hoping for.

Why would you do that? Why would you put your ability to focus on what's most important on automatic hold? Here's what we've observed is usually going on.

When you work for someone else, focus rarely becomes an issue. It's usually defined externally by someone or something else—for example, the company you work for, your boss, and your job description. On your own, what you focus on is all up to you. You have to see the big picture and carve out a piece for yourself, but often we're handicapped in doing this. Most of us live in such a fast-paced, crowded, noisy, and otherwise overly stimulating environment that we've long ago opted to close down or tune out large amounts of sensory input just to cope and maintain our sanity. Having done this for years, it becomes our default setting. We shut out anything other than what's most pressing at the moment.

If you were yelled at repeatedly or abused as a child, you're even more likely than most to put on the blinders, close down, and narrow your perspective as much as possible.

It might seem this narrowing of our sensory field would help us focus on our business, but, paradoxically, it has the opposite effect. It prevents us from getting the big picture that gives us the perspective to see what's most important, to notice the timing of things, and to otherwise relate what we want to do to with what we can do. Without perspective and breadth of information, we can't make good choices. We're left groping in the dark, wishing and hoping but feeling out of control.

The result is a vague sense of impending doom and an undercurrent of fear about what might happen. In an effort to get things under control, we try to do it all. Unfortunately, there is much about being in business for yourself that really is out of our control, so the more controlling we become, the worse things get. And the more we try

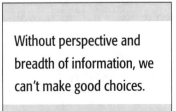

Without perspective and breadth of information, we can't make good choices.

to do, the less we can do because we get too overwhelmed to prioritize, and we close down even more to the input we need. Eventually we may become immobilized with the myriad of demands and possibilities and put our plans on hold.

Warning Signals

When you hear yourself say (or feel like saying) any of the following, know that you're taking on too much, and your ability to see where you fit into the big picture and to discriminate what's most important at the moment has shut down.

"My timing is always off."

"I'm never in the right place at the right time."

"I never seem to do the right thing."

"I can't keep up. I'm not fast enough. "

"I can't concentrate."

"It's not my fault."

"I don't have a choice."

"I can't get my ideas across. I'm misunderstood."

"Everything's out of my control."

"I just can't get it all together."

Reset Suggestions

These are signs that you need to *stop* what you're doing. It's not that you aren't doing enough or doing it fast enough. In trying to control the uncontrollable, you're doing too much too fast. You need to *stop* everything you can and get away, preferably to as quiet and natural a setting as possible to clear your mind and open your senses.

"But," you may be saying, "I can't do that! I have a family to take care of. . . . I have bills to pay. . . . I have responsibilities. . . . I'm already behind."

These "yes, but's" are part and parcel of your default setting. You must get away so you can reset your perspective, tune in to what's most important to you, and begin to put things in order in accord with *your* priorities. Then, instead of using your energy to anticipate what's *going to happen*, look fully at what *is happening* so you can focus your time, money, and energy specifically on what you want to happen.

RX Summary

Discovering Where You Fit

- Focus your attention on your objectives.
- Set priorities.

- Ask what's most important now.
- Set unimportant things aside.
- Shift from worrying to wondering.
- Experiment with acting spontaneously instead of always trying to figure it all out first.

Doing What Needs to Be Done

- Ask yourself, "What am I feeling right now?"
- Be your own silent witness. Step back mentally and observe yourself.
- Start a journal. Reflect on your day, and write your thoughts in your journal.
- Talk or write out your thoughts with others, especially when you feel confused.
- Get a daily planning system (paper or software) to organize your life.
- Break down what you need to do into manageable pieces, and take one step at a time.
- Notice any resistance or difficulty you have to doing these things. What is staying confused and disorganized doing for you?

CAPABILITY 3 — HOLDING YOUR OWN

While the first two hang-ups we've discussed have to do with thinking and planning, this hang-up has to do with taking action. It stops you from acting on your plans. It's about holding yourself back, putting such a drag on your efforts that you can't make any progress. But why would you do this? Why would you hold yourself back? The answer usually lies in the very reason you want to go out on your own in the first place.

Chances are you've been enduring a less than satisfying career situation for some time, maybe even a lifetime. For a while you may have denied there was a problem. At least you've felt stifled in your ability to do anything to change your situation, so you've been sitting on your feelings, holding back your frustration and growing more irritated, anxious, and angry over time because you haven't been doing anything about your dissatisfaction.

To do that all this time, you've had to put a hold on your energy, the very energy that would enable you to take action. You've been enduring instead of acting, and it's become your default position.

Some would say that going out on your own is the ultimate act of self-expression. By cutting your cord to a paycheck, you're saying, "I know who I am. I know what I want, and I know how to get it." But to proceed, you've got to express yourself. You have to take a stand for what you want, draw the line forcefully, and defend your ideas and dreams from others who would impose their opinions, agendas, or will on you.

Of course, you need also to be refreshed and ready to take on whatever each day brings with enthusiasm. You need to know when to be flexible and when to hold your ground, let others know what you want and don't want, and get your message across clearly and effectively without being rigid. Sometimes you will have to confront a situation or even get angry.

But this isn't the way you've been operating, is it? If you've put up and shut up for a long time, if you've been enduring for a long time, you're not practiced at expressing yourself, acting on what you want, and holding your ground. You decided some time ago that doing so wasn't safe or prudent. That would be too scary. And having sat on your desires and feelings for so long, you're probably not feeling refreshed, either. If you refrain from expressing yourself long enough, you become rigid, intense, reactive, impatient, and fault finding. You could even be burned out, running on empty yet still holding yourself back for fear of getting yet another negative, unsupportive response from the world.

If this sounds familiar and you've slipped into feeling dominated and deluged by the demands and "have-to's" imposed by the world, it's a sign that your ability to express yourself and take action is on hold.

Warning Signals

Whenever you hear yourself saying or (feel like saying) the following statements, you're likely operating from your outdated default position of enduring, not taking a stand for what you want to do, and assuming you can't have or act on what you want.

"I can't make this change."
"I'm always behind. I can't seem to get ahead."
"I'm under too much pressure."
"I just can't take this anymore."
"This is just not fair!"
"You have to be really careful."

"This probably won't work out."
"I'm always getting walked on."
"I don't like how things are, but it's not really so bad."
"I can put up with this."
"You have to expect the worst."
Frequent strings of swear words.

Reset Suggestions

It's time to put a name to your fears, look at the problem, and talk about it. You may not want to do that, but that's part of the problem and exactly what you need to do. Express how you feel. That will begin to break the block you're experiencing. You

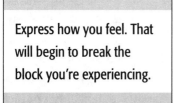

Express how you feel. That will begin to break the block you're experiencing.

might want to write about your feelings in a journal or confide them to a trusted friend.

After you've expressed your feelings, think about them. What are these feelings telling you? What is their meaning? Be willing to change your mind, to view your situation differently and adopt a new perspective. Ask yourself, "What other more productive ways could I look at this?" Seek out other people's points of view. Adopting a new viewpoint will help get you moving. Don't allow yourself to feel justified in holding on to a dysfunctional point of view.

Listen to your frustration, and *take action*. The frustration you're feeling is the pent-up energy you're not using to do what you want to do. Just think how exhausting it is to hold all that energy back day after day. Once you have some insight into your feelings and have considered new points of view, do something—*anything*—that addresses your goals in a positive way. Ask yourself, "What do I *want* to do?" "What *can* I do?" And then, take a deep breath—and keep breathing and start to act and speak out decisively on your plans to go out on your own.

RX Summary

Taking Action on Your Behalf

- Get in touch with what you want and don't want.
- Notice when you're angry about others' rigidity in relating to you.
- Learn how to express your anger effectively.
- Express your positions, needs, and passions clearly.
- Notice when you say you "have to" or fear you "have to" do something.
- Give yourself permission to change your mind.

- Notice when you're overreacting angrily.
- Be willing to hear and understand the viewpoints of others.

Speaking Out for Yourself
- Notice when you're holding your breath.
- Take up a meditative breathing program like yoga or tai chi.
- Engage in a vigorous exercise program for thirty minutes at least three times a week.

> The frustration you're feeling is the pent-up energy you're not using to do what you want to do.

- Notice when you say "I can't" to something you want to do, and ask yourself, "What prevents me from doing that?"
- Notice when life feels like it's closing in, and take action to get the time and space you need.
- Turn your fear and anxiety into action.

CAPABILITY 4 — TAKING CARE OF BUSINESS

Much of creating and running a business of your own is simply handling the nitty-gritty, day-to-day details of getting on with what you want to do with your business. If you can't get yourself to carry out these activities, that's telling you something important. It says that for some reason, you don't think the decision to go on your own is the best move for you. In other words, your heart is not really into it. You're not accepting this new venture. It's not keeping your interest. Instead, you're pushing, dragging, fighting, cajoling, and driving yourself, and it's discouraging because everything seems heavy and harder than it should be. You're just not taking care of business the way you know you should.

Of course, you can draw on a slew of ready-made excuses to explain why you can't do this or that, but if you really wanted to do this, you would. In fact, nothing could stop you from doing it, at least not for long. Yes, of course, you might run into emergencies or crises that would put things on hold for a while, but the moment those passed, you would be right back on track. So why are you sabotaging your efforts?

It could be for any number of reasons, but here's one of the most common ones: Going into business, or the particular business you've chosen, is not for you! It's not what you really want. If what you've chosen to do isn't an expression of who you are at heart, if you don't have a passion for it, if it doesn't get you excited and motivate you, then in the long run you won't do it. Or, you'll do it half-heartedly or at great cost to yourself. So whose idea is this? What makes you think you want to do this? Some typical answers we hear include, "Well, it's a hot business," "I don't know what else to do," or "My husband/wife/friend thought it was a good idea."

Another common reason for this hang-up is that, in your heart, you believe doing what you're trying to do poses a threat to your survival and well-being. Or maybe you've set your goals so high that you feel the need to protect yourself from the hurt and disappointment you fear awaits you when you don't succeed.

If you fail to acknowledge that you don't think it's in your best interest to proceed with your plans, your brain will kick in and unconsciously take control to stop you from doing it. It will do this because we're not designed to function well in unsafe situations. You may drag your feet, run out of energy, get busy, get bogged down in past problems or other people's problems, and blame those things for preventing you from proceeding with your goals. At the extreme, you might unconsciously create a crisis, get a cold or the flu, or otherwise manufacture a "setback" to prevent yourself from proceeding. As long as this effort to protect yourself remains unconscious, you'll end up feeling like the victim, blaming other people and events for your miseries or feeling guilty that you're not doing better.

If you think about it, in many ways, this hang-up is actually a positive thing. It's protecting you. The problem is that by doing it unconsciously, you can't take an objective look at the issues you're concerned about and remove them so you can proceed in a way that would be in your best interest. So, here's the key question: Why would you try to proceed with doing something you don't want to do or don't feel is in your best interest? You probably will want to reset that one.

This default setting is common whenever instead of being appreciated and encouraged for being who you are, you grew up in an environment where no one cared or respected you, and everyone expected you to do what *they* wanted you to do, whether it was in your best interest or not. You may even have been ridiculed, punished, shamed, or ignored when you asserted your own interests. In such circumstances, you may have decided to give up who you are and do what others expect as a way to get along in life. You've probably gotten along okay doing that, but you're not feeling fulfilled. That may be one of the reasons you want to be your own boss.

On your own, however, there's no one to make you do what is expected of you. To succeed, you have to define yourself independently of anyone else's opinions or expectations.

> To succeed, you have to define yourself independently of anyone else's opinions or expectations.

Warning Signals

If you hear yourself saying (or feel like saying) any of the following, know that these are signals that you need to reset your brain and consciously tune into who you really are and what you really want.

"Whatever you say."

"I keep getting stuck in the same old situation."

"My life isn't my own."

"My time's not my own."

"I'm a loser."

"I never get my due. When will my turn come?"

"Something's always holding me back."

"Others get the credit I deserve."

"This is a tough world."

"I better watch out."

"Nothing's happening."

"Everything's out of sync."

"I hate rejection."

"I hate criticism."

"I'm just doing the best I can."

Reset Suggestions

These are all signals that you've disconnected from what we call your inner compass, the capacity to know what you want and don't want in life and when you're on the right track and when you're not. If you've put yourself and who you are on hold, reset your default for your inner compass. Ask yourself, "Is this really for *me*? Who am I, really? What do *I* want? What's best for *me*?" Remember these:

Three Ways to Go Nowhere
- Focus on the past.
- Blame the past.
- Focus on other people's problems.

So, give up concentrating on past problems. Let others handle their problems; they can do it. If you want to make a change, you have to focus your attention on what's best for you now. Take a look at your goals. Are you expecting too much of yourself right now? What would be the right amount of activity and effort for you right now? Are you putting your survival in jeopardy by going out on your own? How could you arrange to handle your start-up costs and living expenses (see chapter 4) to safeguard your security?

You'll find that once you've found a business that you're excited and eager to leap out of bed to do, adjusted your goals to fit what you can manage without strain, and have a secure entry plan, your resistance to taking care of business should melt away.

> If you want to make a change, you have to focus your attention on what's best for you now.

RX Summary

Commanding Respect
- Notice your own likes, dislikes, and needs and how they differ from others'.
- Try doing things differently than usual to see how you like it.
- Set aside time for yourself each day, even if it's only a few minutes.
- Open a bank account just for yourself. Put something no matter how small in it each month.
- Take a position, even if it feels uncomfortable, and defend it.
- Set boundaries on your time, money, and energy.
- Say no to things you don't want to do.

Releasing the Brakes
- Create a place for yourself where you'll be appreciated.
- Participate fully in what you do.
- Relax and let things flow.
- Look for the good in life.

Attracting Success Without Distress

- Find and let the good stuff into your life each day. At the end of the day, note at least five things you've enjoyed and feel grateful for.
- Notice when you're resisting life. Accept what is and move on to what can be.
- Get involved with what you love.
- Open yourself to the flow of life.
- Try meditation programs that enable you to feel peace and harmony each day, and carry this feeling into your life. Notice when that feeling leaves and why so you can take action to allow your life to flow more harmoniously.

Protecting Your Assets

- Notice when you don't feel safe. Check out whether you are presently in danger or whether something in the present is reminding you of sometime in the past.
- Take conscious action to protect yourself.
- Put yourself in safe situations.
- Set reasonable goals you know you can accomplish, and build on those.
- Initiate specific active steps toward what you're seeking in life.
- Don't push too hard; just let it happen.

All Talk, No Action: Is It Me? Do I Have Hang-Ups! Part II

CAPABILITY 5 —
GOING FOR WHAT YOU WANT

Like it or not, most of us live in a crowded, highly competitive world in which simply hanging out your shingle, passing out a few business cards, putting up a Web site, or taking out an ad will not bring in the business you need to support yourself. To enjoy a steady flow of business, we must spread the word about what we have to offer in memorable and impactful ways that attract attention, inspire confidence, and motivate action.

So, what is the difference between a person who draws flocks of eager clients and another who goes unnoticed and overlooked despite trying to attract business? Of course, it's having something to offer that people want or need. But assuming that, how do they know to choose you and not someone else? The answer can't be found in advertising hype, clever word games, or tricky sales techniques. Nor is it even the quality of the work

> To enjoy a steady flow of business, we must spread the word about what we have to offer in memorable and impactful ways that attract attention, inspire confidence, and motivate action.

you do. No one can experience the quality of your work until people have had the opportunity to experience it. Unfortunately, as you may know all too painfully, sometimes the best technicians or craftspeople languish while far less skilled and talented individuals thrive.

What makes the difference? The answer is personal power, that personal charisma that causes someone to pause and take note of your message, even when it's not delivered in person. We each have it, but we don't all use it. Often that's because we don't understand or appreciate our own brand of personal power.

In our society, we tend to think of personal power as that sense of showmanship that makes for the dynamic salesperson—Tony Robbins personified. True, this is one form of personal power. But it's not the only one. There is the personal power of quiet sophistication. There's jovial, humorous personal power. Forceful, authoritative personal power. Warm and caring personal power. Our personal power is as individual as our fingerprints and as varied and original as the crystalline patterns of a snowflake.

Personal power is what makes us stand out from the crowd. It's what draws the people to us with whom we'll work best while repelling those who aren't so well suited to our style. As with anything else that we want to grow and develop, we must plant ourselves and our business firmly in fertile soil among those who welcome and appreciate who we are and what we have to offer.

Left to your natural instincts, you would do the following:

- *Gravitate to arenas where you and your business can shine.* When you're self-employed, virtually every decision you make—from choosing a business that's suited to you to selecting marketing methods you enjoy and establishing a schedule that suits your needs—will either enhance your natural style and abilities (and thereby your business) or encumber them. So the natural tendency would be to set yourself up in situations that you handle well and that will support you in being fully who you are.

- *Readily recognize situations and activities that will and won't support you.* You won't want to waste your time beating your head against a stone wall or endure the bashing of repeated rejections. Attempting to market in barren fields, for example, sets you up for failure, as does trying to use marketing methods you feel unsure or uncomfortable with.

> As with anything else that we want to grow and develop, we must plant ourselves and our business firmly in fertile soil among those who welcome and appreciate who we are and what we have to offer.

- *Turn what you've got into what you want.* Nearly everyone has limitations on their time, money, energy, and talents, but we also each have at least *some* of all these things. Accessing our personal power enables us to utilize our existing circumstances to create what we want.

- *Find the balance between being pushy and being a pushover.* Obviously, to get and do business, you must make an impression on others. If you're too pushy, however, they are turned off; but if you're too timid, you become a pushover and end up giving far more than you're getting.

The desirability of doing these things probably seems obvious, yet concerns about having to sell and promote one's business and ask for money comprise the most common reason people abandon the idea of being their own boss. They have hang-ups about selling themselves, and they're afraid they won't be able to attract enough business. Why is that?

If you love what you do, believe people can benefit from it, and know you can do it well, why wouldn't you leap out of bed in the morning, raring to find people who want and need what you can provide? Why would talented and otherwise capable people put a hold on the very personal power, or charisma, that would draw business to them naturally without hype or manipulation? Let's take a closer look at the most common possibilities in the following sections.

People Pleasers

If you were repeatedly rejected, punished, or made fun of when you exuberantly expressed your personal power, your default position in life may be People Pleaser. In your desire to please everyone and offend no one, you may be afraid to unleash your distinctive style of personal power, preferring to articulate what you have to offer in such innocuous and commonplace ways that no one takes note. But it's virtually impossible to be appreciated, let alone sought after, if you don't distinguish or define yourself sufficiently to attract those who find who you are or what you offer appealing. Of course, that will turn away those who don't, but why would you want to waste your time trying to attract them?

> In your desire to please everyone and offend no one, you may be afraid to unleash your distinctive style of personal power.

Hypersensitive Pessimists

If you've come to believe that people won't pay attention to you no matter what you do, chances are you will approach them with caution instead of confidence. If every slight is taken personally as a painful reminder of your inadequacy, you may be hypersensitive to possible rejection and unable to pick up the subtle cues that would tell you who is genuinely interested in what you have to offer and who is not. On the other hand, to overcome the presumed resistance you anticipate, you may be overly aggressive, come on too strong, and turn people off.

We've all met pushy salespeople or companies that hype themselves shamelessly. If you think that's what it takes, that's what you'll try to do. You'll become a caricature of someone else instead of finding the subtle balance between making a bold enough statement to make a unique positive impression and being so in-their-face that people are turned off.

Hopeless Pessimists

If your early life experiences convinced you that you're not going to get what you want no matter what you do, you probably won't be motivated to get out and try to get business. Why try? You've put your personal power in mothballs. Just the thought of marketing may deenergize and depress you, although you may not know why, attributing your feelings to other things (e.g., "I'm just not feeling up to it today").

Tolerators

If you've had to stomach a lot of unpleasant situations throughout your life that you couldn't do anything about, chances are you don't put much stock in your personal power. Instead, you've probably taken a prescriptive approach to marketing, doing what you've read or been told is the thing to do. As long as that happens to work for you, you're okay. But marketing is usually an experimental process that's honed by trial and error. So when the prescribed methods you've been doing by rote don't work, you may feel overwhelmed by the prospect of marketing. Or, since you're pretty good at ignoring your problems or pretending they don't exist, you may not notice that your marketing efforts aren't working and feel bewildered about why you're not getting business.

Warning Signals

Whenever you hear yourself saying, or feel like saying, any of the following, know that your personal power is on hold:

"No one seems to appreciate me and my work."

"Why do they get all the business?"

"Why is this such a struggle? I've had it."

"They're not going to push me around."

"Business is a bummer."

"You can't change the way things are."

"I can never win, no matter what I do."

"There's no use trying; I won't get what I want anyway."

"After all I've done . . ."

"This probably isn't going to work out."

"What am I doing wrong?"

"I can't deal with this."

"Whatever I do is never enough."

"There's nothing funny about this."

"I can't *do* this!"

Reset Suggestions

If you're not optimistic and enthusiastic about raising funds, marketing, or selling your products or services, you've put your personal power on hold. You are biologically designed to go for what you want. Desire, action, satisfaction. That's the natural process you were born equipped to follow. We have a desire, we take action to meet it by creating or finding the right circumstances, and then we feel the satisfaction of fulfilling our desire.

> We have a desire, we take action to meet it by creating or finding the right circumstances, and then we feel the satisfaction of fulfilling our desire.

So, notice where your cycle breaks down. Have you shut down your belief that you can have what you want? Are you failing to find circumstances in which you and your business will be appreciated? Have you resigned yourself to settle for less?

If so, you're on an automatic mind-set of "hide and hope" or "push and pray." You're hanging out in the woodwork and hoping someone will notice who you are and the value of what you have to offer, just venturing out every so often with your hat in trembling hand. Or maybe you're coming on like gangbusters to overcome all the resistance you expert to get.

It's time to unleash your personal power. Reset your mind to "broadcast and attract." You're not dependent on someone else to get where you want to go. Connect with your belief in your own value. Your value isn't determined by others. So express yourself fully so people who are attracted to what you offer can find you. Broadcast who you are and what you're doing in places and through media suited to your strengths.

Reach out to those who have a need or interest in your business. Don't concern yourself with those who don't. Would you go looking for an iced cold drink when you need something to warm you up? Would you bemoan not finding a cold drink when you need a hot one? Of course not.

Start looking for the people who are looking for you. Make sure your antennae are up and that your broadcast signal is loud and clear as to just who you are and who you can best serve. This won't be a struggle, because it will come naturally to you. If what you're doing feels like a struggle, it's not *you*. Notice the difference between when and where you feel comfortable and when you do not. Notice when things feel easy and natural. That's *you*.

Acknowledge your own worthiness, and refuse to settle for less. Welcome whatever feedback you get so you can focus your message even more clearly on those who will welcome and appreciate you and your business.

RX Summary

Being Appreciated for Who You Are
- Notice when you're feeling persecuted.
- Notice when you're putting up with things that aren't in your best interest.
- Make a list of the things in your life that irritate you, and take action to get rid of them.
- Appreciate the value of your contributions, and don't get into situations where others discount them.

Taking Problems in Stride
- Ask yourself from moment to moment, "What am I really feeling?"
- Notice what makes you laugh, what gives you joy, and what leaves you more energized after you've done it. Do more of those things.
- Notice when and why you avoid doing the things you enjoy.
- Watch comedies.
- Spend a morning, afternoon, day, or weekend doing only whatever you want to do.
- Get away for a retreat to a location where you can enjoy yourself.

Being Up to the Challenge
- Cut back on or stop drinking coffee and other caffeinated beverages.
- Stop avoiding conflicts either by ignoring them or by browbeating others into giving in.
- Stop trying to control everything. Have confidence in yourself and others to resolve things so everyone wins.
- Instead of pushing to make things happen, explore and let them happen.

Handling Whatever Comes Along
- Notice when you're happy and when you're not. Notice what you need to do to have more happiness.
- Notice when you're feeling overwhelmed, and break things down into manageable pieces.
- Notice when things don't feel right, and ask, "What can I do about it?"
- Take the time to digest whatever is happening in your life.

Turning What You've Got into What You Want
- Take a rejuvenating vacation or retreat, even if it's only for an afternoon or weekend.
- Become aware of what you really want in life.
- Figure out what you think is preventing you from having what you really want, and make decisions to do something about getting it.
- Whenever you hear yourself complaining or blaming others for holding you back, take action instead to do something about it.
- Don't wait for others to solve your problems. Start today to solve them yourself.
- Notice when you're irritated or depressed. Ask yourself what's bothering you, and take action to do something about it.

CAPABILITY 6—GIVING YOUR BEST

Being self-employed is essentially a creative process, and we humans are essentially creative beings. So self-employment is truly an optimal milieu for us. As your own boss, you are an artist, turning ideas and desires into realities, creating something that didn't exist from the raw materials of time, money, energy, and other resources. These are your artist's tools. But even on your own, you can't create in isolation. You create in connection with others, with the marketplace, the times you live in, your community, and your field.

In researching her book *The Meaning of Work Among the Self-Employed* (Human Sciences Department, Institute, 1994), which is about what motivates people to become self-employed, Dr. Barrie Jaeger found that the freedom to create is high on the list. Many of those she interviewed talked of the blissful feelings they have when immersed fully in the work they love. This feeling of connection or unity, which is independent of time and space, has been described eloquently by the renowned educator Mihaly Csikszentmihalyi in his classic book *Flow: The Psychology of Optimal Experience* (Harper-Perennial, 1990).

While in the creative process, we're in the flow—in the groove, so to speak. At such times, life is like a symphony; we're moving in sync and functioning at our best. Anything seems possible. Even problems become welcome challenges that don't break our stride. Often in this state we surprise and delight ourselves with what we can create. But when our creativity is blocked, we're not at our best, and things usually don't flow. We feel stuck or swept away; nothing seems to work, and nothing seems possible.

Creativity lives on a narrow thread between independence and dependence. If you are too independent, you cut yourself off from the vibrant web of life that links you to the world, and you and your business lose your relevance. On the other hand, if you are too dependent on others for approval and support, that's when you get swept away by others' agendas and lose yourself and your inner compass. Either way, your creativity suffers, and you can't do your best.

> Creativity lives on a narrow thread between independence and dependence.

But, with all the power and delights of the creative process available to you as part of your human biology, why would you shut down your creativity? The following sections consider four of the most common reasons we put ourselves on automatic disconnect.

Trapped in Past Losses

If you've had a history of loss or of having things being taken from you, you may fear that you'll lose anything good that comes your way, so why try for it? Why subject yourself to yet another traumatic loss? If you don't try, you can never lose anything you value, even if that means having less than you'd like to in life. Great unresolved losses also steal your energy; you're just too tired to create anew, and you feel unworthy.

If this is your situation, you might be excited and energized at first by your plans to go out on your own, but as you get closer to actually doing so, you may begin to lose energy for your ideas and get stuck instead in thinking that you don't have what it takes to create what you want.

Trapped in Past Rejections

Some people mistakenly turn to self-employment after profound disappointments on the job. They think that on their own they won't need anyone else and can escape the pain and hassle of working with others. If in the past you've been rejected repeatedly when you risked sharing your creativity, you may have concluded you'd prefer to go it alone. But, while it's true that as your own boss you can pick with whom you will and won't work, creating a business is always a joint venture. You are creating through your connections with clients or customers, suppliers, employees (if you have them), referral sources, colleagues, and others. If you've set yourself on automatic disconnect, you may find yourself feeling apathetic about getting your business under way; on the other hand, you're also probably feeling frustrated about being stuck in a rut. At this point you may start to feel like giving up.

> While it's true that as your own boss you can pick with whom you will and won't work, creating a business is always joint venture.

Taking on Too Much

While the two previous default positions are about disconnecting from others and losing the creative energy that connection brings, this hang-up and the one that follows are about getting so enmeshed in the needs of others that your own desires get swept aside. If you're one of those people who take on more than you can handle—including doing things you don't want to do—in order to be accepted, your family will love you, your clients and customers will love you, but you will probably end up too overwhelmed to do your best.

To cope, you may be loading up on coffee or taking various medications or other remedies to give yourself a boost so you can keep going as if everything's okay, but it's not. You may have already found yourself cutting corners and patching together short-term fixes to get by, but barely.

You may be feeling confused about your lack of success because you're such an enthusiastic and positive person. But you're the one who's losing out, because in the long run you are shortchanging everyone by not being able to offer your best to yourself or to others.

Ignoring Difficulties

Business is replete with challenges that must be confronted, and our natural human response would be to confront and resolve them creatively. But if you grew up in an environment where you were punished when you pointed out obvious problems, or if confronting problems around your house just made matters worse, then you may be afraid to confront the challenges that going out on your own presents. You may have learned to just suck it up and ignore major problems, accepting that they're just part of life.

You can't be at your best while living with problems that are sapping your energy and blocking your progress. And, of course, if you ignore your problems, you won't tap into your creativity to solve them. So, instead you may find yourself procrastinating, avoiding and putting off what you'd rather not deal with, and wondering why you're not able to make the progress you would expect of yourself.

Warning Signals

Whenever you hear yourself saying, or feel like saying, any of the following, know that you've blocked your creativity from kicking in and that is limiting your ability to do your best.

"I need a drink/cigarette (etc.)."   "Sigh! Sigh."

"I just don't get it."

"I'm fine." (when you're not)
"Everything's fine." (when it's not)
"Nothing I do ever works."
"Why should I even try?"
"I'm stuck in a rut."
"No one takes me into account."

"I just can't get a handle on what's wrong."
"I keep putting off what I need to do."
"I'm a loner."
"I can't do anything about my problems."
"People are trouble."
"I can't finish my projects."

Reset Suggestions

If you're stuck and can't seem to do what you know you're capable of, it means that you're blocking your creativity, and it's time to take a look at the past to find the default setting that's put your creativity on hold. Is it a history of loss or rejection and disappointment? If so, you will need to heal the wounds of those experiences so you can dare to risk again. This may be a difficult task, because to heal these wounds, you will need to feel the pain they've brought you so you can let it go. That may not seem possible or desirable to you.

> The remarkable thing about painful feelings is that when finally expressed, they do pass, and chances are you won't be able to succeed in your new business until they do.

But the remarkable thing about painful feelings is that when finally expressed, they do pass, and chances are you won't be able to succeed in your new business until they do. You owe it to yourself to resolve these blocks. You should not have to live your life enslaved to the past. There are no guarantees of success. Life does involve loss, rejection, and disappointment at times, but there is so much more. By blocking your creative energy, you are robbing yourself of the greatest joys that comprise the rest of life.

If, to succeed, you're taking on so much that you can't do your best, look at why you're choosing to let your connections with others sweep you off your own course. What's the worst thing that would happen if you began setting better boundaries for what you will and won't do? Could you live with whatever that might be?

Or are you afraid to confront major problems that are blocking your progress? Are you ignoring them? Putting them off? Procrastinating? What's the worst thing that would happen if you brought them out in the open? Not dealing with them is not getting you anywhere. And it won't. Of course, it's possible you'll displease someone. It may even be unpleasant for a time while you resolve the issues. However, once you're free to use your creativity to deal with whatever situations await you, you'll be free to get on with your life.

Because all these particular issues are often buried in painful past experiences, you may find it useful to work through them with a counselor, therapist, or healer. Other things that might help include regular meditation, massage, daily exercise to the point of sweating, and drinking enough water.

RX Summary

Having What It Takes
- Get moving. Begin a regular exercise program. Notice and explore any resistance you have to exercising.
- Notice and process past grief or loss you're still carrying with you.
- Connect with your big dreams and anything that prevents you from thinking you're worthy or able to pursue them.

Remaining Both Excited and Realistic
- Become aware of the qualities you have above and beyond all your roles and the particular activities you engage in.
- Notice how, when, and why you overload yourself with more than you can handle.
- Learn to say no when your plate is full.
- Refrain from using alcohol, drugs, or overeating.
- Notice when you want to turn to these substances to numb yourself to how you feel.
- Notice what you're feeling at those times, and ask yourself how you could eliminate the sources of pain and discomfort from your life.

Taking on Too Much
- Drink enough water every day. To determine how much, divide your body weight in half. That's the number of ounces you should be drinking.
- Confront your fears.
- Face unpleasant problems in your life and confront them.
- Stop avoiding the issues that are messing up your life.

Creating with Others
- Cultivate a take-it-or-leave it attitude.
- Notice when you're disconnecting from others and why.
- Notice when you're off in your own world.
- Notice when you give up on something you actually still want.

CAPABILITY 7 — THE STRENGTH TO MAKE IT

Okay, failure can definitely be a hang-up, especially if you've failed before. Sometimes it's our fear of failing that hangs us up (see Capability 3—Holding Your Own), but some people actually do fail. Surely there may have been external causes of failure that were beyond your control (e.g., a downturn in the economy, a change in legislation that wipes out your field, the announcement of new technology that makes what you do obsolete). There are also mistakes one can make and learn from the next time around (e.g., not doing enough marketing, running out of money because you didn't have an adequate entry plan, spending yourself into the ground). These can become building blocks for success.

Al Neuharth, founder of *USA Today,* is remembered as saying, "If you're over thirty and haven't failed really big at least once, you'd better hurry because time is running out." There's basis to this observation. In research for her book *Skills for Success* (Ballantine Books, 1996), Adele Scheele found that successful people have more failures than unsuccessful people. The reason: Successful people experiment more. Rich Minitir, who has interviewed hundreds of entrepreneurs, says, "What makes America great is not just our freedom to succeed, but our freedom to fail. Only in America is failing a credential—in other countries (such as Britain, Russia, Japan), if you make a mistake, you're finished; here, your entrepreneurial experience either way is an asset." (See his article "Entrepreneurial Parents Profit from More Time with the Kids," *Reader's Digest* [August 1999].)

Obviously failure doesn't have to be a hang-up because, on the one hand, there are those things you can't do anything about other than just fold up and start anew, and, on the other hand, there are those things you can do better

> Failure doesn't have to be a hang-up because, on the one hand, there are those things you can't do anything about other than just fold up and start anew, and, on the other hand, there are those things you can do better next time.

next time. But what about the other things? If you're prone to fail again and again, what is this about? That's where failure becomes a hang-up.

In business, everything is constantly changing, and we have to change with it. But we can't change if we don't admit that things aren't working. A couple who started a referral service comes to mind. They hired a consultant to help them develop a business plan. The plan looked good, and they had a great deal of confidence in the consultant. They quickly signed up lots of vendors who happily paid a reasonable fee to be listed with their service, but that reasonable fee was based on charging customers who used the service marginal fees as well. That's where the problems started.

The customers would not pay for referrals. They thought a referral service was a great idea and liked the possibility of using one, but when it came to paying a few dollars for each referral, they just wouldn't do it.

The couple continued to market and market and market, convinced that if they could just reach enough of the right people, their business would be fine. But as time passed, more and more friends and colleagues began to suggest that they needed to change their plan. Boost the fees for the vendors, and eliminate the fee for the users, folks suggested. "No," they said, "if we just keep marketing, we'll make it!"

They had confidence. They had determination. They had persistence. All traits every entrepreneur needs. But they ended up having to declare bankruptcy because they wouldn't change. They had fallen in love with their business plan. It's like having a lover who's no good for you, but you can't give him or her up. They hated their situation, but they couldn't let go of the plan they'd invested so much money in developing. And they were angry—angry at the stingy public who wouldn't pay their marginal fee and angry at their friends and colleagues who disagreed with them about sticking with the plan.

Upon questioning, they admitted something like this had happened before—more than once, in fact. Of course, the details were different, but the process and the results were the same, so when the referral business went under, once again, they felt like failures.

Now consider this story: A college professor believed he had been fired unjustly. Although he loved his job, he had actually been thinking for a number of years about leaving to start his own specialty consulting firm. It would be more lucrative and provide him with greater flexibility to enjoy his family. So, he saw the fact he'd been let go by the college as an opportunity and began making plans to start his firm. At the same time, he was so angry about having been let go unjustly that he decided to file a lawsuit. The lawsuit dragged out for years and drained him emotionally, physically, and financially to the point that he was unable to make a success of his consulting firm. Eventually broken and filled with hatred, he developed a number of physical illnesses and became disabled. But he never gave up the lawsuit. It remains active to this day.

> As long as we can't change and won't get rid of or away from what isn't working in our lives, we will continue to fail chronically at pursuing our intentions.

This hang-up is about holding on to harmful things that aren't working while struggling to get away from them until ultimately they pull you under and you fail. As long as we can't change and won't get rid of or away from what isn't working in our lives, we will continue to fail chronically at pursuing our intentions. If we hate the way something's going, the natural response is to *change*. It could be the job we hate but can't leave; the clients we hate but won't discharge; the travel for our business that we hate but won't discontinue; the business partner who's destroying the company but we won't part with.

Hating a situation is the result of getting involved with something or someone in error. It might have seemed like a good thing at one time, and maybe it was a good thing for a while, but at some point it is no longer any good for us. The hatred we feel toward this person or situation is designed to motivate us to extricate ourselves from such mistakes, to get rid of or away from them, not to hold on to them. Chronic pain, discomfort, and unhappiness are always signs that we need to get rid of something old and/or to head off toward something new.

Why would you stop your natural response to rid your life of something you hate? Generally, it's because you've learned to live with misery. Often it's because you were too young or otherwise unable to do anything about miserable circumstances. Sometimes, as in the case of the lawsuit, it looks like you're fighting against a miserable situation, but actually it's become a tar baby that keeps you mired in it.

Warning Signals

If you hear yourself saying, or wanting to say, any of the following, know you are blocking your innate ability to get rid of something or someone harmful to your success:

"I've just got to put up with this."

"I know this is bad, but I can't imagine things being otherwise."

"You can't trust anything that seems really good."

"Life is hard. There's always a lot you have to put up with."

"As bad as it is, it's not that bad; I can take it."

"Something always sabotages my best efforts."

"Life seems to work against me."

"There's nothing I can do about it."

"I have to do this. I don't have a choice."

Reset Suggestions

If you're holding on to things that are pulling you under, *you need a change.* Take an inventory of the things you hate about your current situation. Then create a list of all the reasons you have to hold on to these things. These are each part of a dysfunctional default setting. They aren't working! They are excuses you use to stay in this default position. Sometime in the past, you turned off your natural inborn ability to reject or get away from things that are working against you. Now, turn it back on.

Of course, there may be consequences when you do so, but you are strong. Really strong. Just think of all you've been enduring. You can almost certainly endure the fallout of improving your life, especially if your other abilities, discussed earlier, are reset so that you can call on them to confront, to protect, to create—in short, to help develop the life you want.

If you have a number of things you hate, prioritize your list. Begin with the most detrimental to your well-being and start eliminating them one by one. Then turn up your sensitivity to negativity. The earlier you notice things that detract from your life and your success, the less drain you will experience and the more flexible and able you'll be to make changes in your best interest.

But, you may say, isn't this being selfish? In fact, it is not. What works best for your health and well-being is what works best in the overall scheme of things. When we honor ourselves and our abilities, the result is a better world.

CAROLYN'S STORY, CONTINUED

Carolyn recognized herself as the classic case of someone who learned to live with misery. As a child, she lived with her mother and her disabled grandmother. Her parents had divorced before she was old enough to remember her father, with whom she had only recently reconnected. The grandmother's illness dominated their household. Carolyn wasn't allowed to make noise, have friends over, or do anything a child might spontaneously want to do. She was even punished sternly for crying, as it would wake up or upset her ailing grandmother. Her mother took in sewing, and it was Carolyn's job to care for her grandmother when she wasn't at school so that her mother could work.

After her grandmother died, Carolyn went to college on a scholarship and met her future husband. She dropped out of school to marry and, for a few years, she enjoyed what she considered an ideal life as a wife and mother to their two daughters. Then, while her daughters were still young, her husband was killed in an automobile accident. Desperate to support herself and her daughters and with no job experience, she took a low-paying position as an assistant manager in one of a chain of eldercare facilities. When the manager at her facility left, she was given responsibility for his duties as well as her own without a pay increase.

RX Summary

- Notice people and situations that are toxic to you.
- Recognize when you are feeling pain from your circumstances.
- Express how you feel.

As she considered her situation, Carolyn could see how she was continuing in her mother's footsteps by putting her responsibilities for others over her own needs. She recognized she had virtually no experience with acting on what she wanted. Actually, she had no idea what she wanted, so she could not understand how her colleagues were able to see potential in her situation that she couldn't. She could also see that she was a pushover. She didn't really know how to hold her ground and wasn't even sure what ground she would want to hold. As competent as she was at managing her household and the eldercare facility, she was unsure of her ability to turn the opportunities her colleagues offered into a secure income for her family.

Carolyn acknowledged she was a People Pleaser, a Hopeless Pessimist, and a Tolerator, and she desperately wanted to reset her reactions so she could stop focusing on other people's problems and start facing and expressing her feelings so she could begin to make changes.

But how? These patterns were so ingrained that she easily slipped back into thinking there was nothing she could do about her situation. After all, she explained, "I'm a widow. I have two young girls to support, and my father needs me now. I don't have a college degree, and the consulting field is very competitive. "

- Ask yourself what you can do about it.
- Take steps to get away from or eliminate negative circumstances that aren't working in your life.
- Notice when you blame others, and take responsibility for taking care of yourself in the situation.

Question 3: How Do I Reset My Settings?

Usually simply becoming aware of your hang-ups will not free you from them. Because they are held in place by your mental default settings, the moment you go on with your life, they will kick back in automatically until you reset them. Unfortunately, unlike with your computer, you can't simply click off a default setting with the flick of a mouse. To change your outdated mental default settings, you have to reprogram your mind. But there are two ways to do that: Mental Monitoring and Sensory Revalidation. They are both effective reprogramming tools. The question is, Which one is best suited to you? Which one are you more likely to follow through on?

When using Mental Monitoring, you reprogram your responses by consciously monitoring your dysfunctional reactions, stopping them midcycle, and then immediately doing something different over and over until a new neural pathway is established. It's a very *left-brain* approach. In using Sensory Validation, you do specific sensory-based activities on a daily basis that reset your reactions subconsciously, and at some point you automatically begin to react differently. It's a very *right-brain* approach.

MENTAL MONITORING

Constance vigilance is the key to this form of reprogramming the reactions that are keeping you stuck. You consciously set out to notice the Warning Signals and reset them to the desired behaviors we described earlier.

To use this method, follow these steps:

1. Select the most problematic capability you wish to reset based on the earlier survey. For Carolyn, that would be Capability 7—The Strength to Make It.

2. Post the appropriate Warning Signals in your home and office where you will see them frequently. For Carolyn, those are as follows:

"Life seems to work against me."

"I know this is bad, but I can't imagine things being otherwise."

"Something always sabotages my best efforts."

"You can't trust anything that seems really good."

"As bad as it is, it's not that bad; I can take it."

"I've just got to put up with this."

"There's nothing I can do about it."

"Life is hard. There's always a lot you have to put up with."

"I have to do this. I don't have a choice."

Your goal is to monitor yourself so you become aware of any time you say, or feel like saying, any of these signals.

3. Review the Reset Suggestions to identify the one(s) best suited to the setting you need to reprogram. Then post the RX Summary beside your list of Warning Signals. For Carolyn, these are as follows:

- Notice people and situations that are toxic to you.
- Recognize when you are feeling pain from your circumstances.
- Express how you feel.
- Ask yourself what you can do about it.
- Take steps to get away from or eliminate negative circumstances that aren't working in your life.
- Notice when you blame others, and take responsibility for taking care of yourself in the situation.

These are the new default reactions that will replace your dysfunctional settings.

4. Whenever you become aware of yourself saying or feeling like saying any of the Warning Signals, *stop* whatever you're thinking or doing and replace it with a new thought and behavior from the RX Summary.

The goal is to *do something different* each time you are about to react from your outdated default position. For Carolyn, when someone needs her to do something that would prevent her from going ahead with her plans and she hears herself thinking, "Well, I have to do this. I don't have a choice," she needs to *stop* and:

- identify her feelings;
- recognize that dropping her plans again will be toxic to her;
- ask herself what she could do differently; and
- make arrangements that will account for her needs.

As you can see, you will need to self-monitor your thoughts and reactions relentlessly to use this method effectively. Of course, you won't catch yourself every time. You will miss some, probably many. That's okay. Yes, you did it again, but identifying what you did after the fact will help you be more alert next time. In time the new behaviors will become the default reactions, and you will begin to use the new behaviors automatically.

> In time the new behaviors will become the default reactions, and you will begin to use the new behaviors automatically.

Once you have successfully reset this first capability, go on to another of the hang-ups you identified, if any.

Many people love this method because it makes them feel like they're in control, and they know exactly how well they're doing from day to day. Learning occurs from the conscious to the unconscious. It works much like learning a golf or tennis swing from an instructor. The instructor tells you how to do it. It doesn't feel natural, because it's not how you're accustomed to swinging. You have to concentrate on your swing instead of just enjoying the game. But as you practice, eventually you master the swing and will be free to concentrate on your game.

Other people really dislike this method, however. For them, it takes away the spontaneity of life. They don't like continually monitoring their every thought and feeling. For them it feels very cumbersome and unnatural. They'll probably prefer Sensory Revalidation.

SENSORY REVALIDATION

Whereas Mental Monitoring requires you to focus on your hang-ups, Sensory Revalidation requires just the opposite. You don't think about your hang-ups at all. Once a day you step completely outside your normal life and do a sensory repatterning activity. These activities and the philosophy underpinning them are based on basic principles of ecopsychology developed by educational psychologist Dr. Michael Cohen.

This method starts from the assumption that the mental default settings that are hanging you up are distortions of what

> This method starts from the assumption that the mental default settings that are hanging you up are distortions of what you, as a human being, would do naturally.

you, as a human being, would do naturally. Biologically you have the specific innate capabilities you need to react in ways that will further your well-being and the well-being of all around you. These innate abilities include all seven of the capabilities needed to start your new business.

You have the capability to know what is safe and unsafe for you to do at any moment, for example, as well as what is toxic and what is nurturing to you. But this knowing is not primarily mental in the sense that it's composed of words and thoughts learned from others. In fact, initially this innate wisdom is sensory and nonverbal in nature. By reconnecting in primal, nonverbal, sensory ways with your own natural wisdom, you revalidate it and automatically reset your mental programming, freeing your natural capabilities.

So, instead of learning consciously by reprogramming your mind mentally until you eventually act in new ways unconsciously, with Sensory Revalidation you reprogram your mind unconsciously through sensory experiences. Then, by reflecting on these experiences, you bring the learning into consciousness and begin to notice the desired changes you've made.

To use this method, you will jot notes in a notebook or journal each day. Select the most problematic capability you wish to reset based on the survey in chapter 6, and write it in the front of your notebook so you will know what to compare future mental and behavioral changes with. Again, for Carolyn, that was Capability 7—The Strength to Make It.

Initial Activities

Begin with the following three activities:

1. Pinch your arm until you notice your body telling you to stop because it feels uncomfortable and unpleasant. This is an example of your innate intelligence in operation. Not a word was spoken, yet your body knew how to signal you what to do. Can you trust this sensory wisdom to inform you when you need to act?

2. Hold your breath. Notice when your body tells you to breathe again. Note what sensations in your body are telling you that it's time to take a breath. Notice that your body will not let you stop breathing. You have a built-in default setting that keeps you breathing. You will actually pass out before you can asphyxiate yourself. Notice how uncomfortable you become when you don't allow yourself to follow the natural urge to breathe. Now take a breath and notice how pleasurable it feels to breathe normally again. That feeling is how nature rewards us when we act to fill our needs.

3. To do this third activity, go to **www.JustAskaTree.com** and click on **Color Test**. For the best results, don't proceed with this activity until you are there. Then say out loud the colors of the words you see on the screen.

- Did you say the names of the font colors, or did you say the words? Because our culture is so language oriented, most people will read the words rather than report on the colors. But consider when you learned to recognize the color green. Could you recognize the color green before you learned the word for it?
- If you read the words, repeat the activity by saying aloud the names of the font colors. Now, notice the feeling you have as you say the font colors out loud. Take particular note of the difference between how you feel when your say the word *green* that's written in green on the screen and when you say the other ink colors that do not match their words.
- Where in your body do your feel this difference? How would you describe the different feelings or sensations? For purposes of communication, let's call the feeling you have when you said the word *green* in the green font the Green/Green feeling, and the feeling you have

when you read the other font colors that don't match with their words, the Green/Orange feeling.

- We are biologically attracted to Green/Green experiences. This Green/Green feeling is the voice of the inner compass. It tells us, "*Yes.* This is good. This is okay." The Green/Orange tells us, "*No.*" We are guided away from Green/Orange experiences by the often subtle but distinctively unsettling feeling they produce.

- The Green/Orange feeling is how your body lets you know there is an incongruity between your innate sensory wisdom and what you've been taught or learned to think and believe. In other words, it's the sensory, nonverbal signal that a dysfunctional mental default setting is at work, stopping you from doing what your innate intelligence would guide you toward.

- Reflect on these activities. What meaning do they have for you? What are the three most important things you learned from these activities? Write your reflections and learnings in your journal.

Daily Activity

Allow one night's sleep before proceeding to the following exercise. From that point on, do the following exercise at some time during each day:

1. Notice how you feel physically and mentally before you start this exercise.

2. Go outdoors to one of the most natural areas that's accessible to you. (You may use different areas from day to day.) The more natural, the better. If you don't have a particularly natural setting nearby, you might choose your yard, a garden, a potted plant, an aquarium, or even a pet.

3. Find something natural in this area that is attractive to you. It could be a tree, a flower, a sensation, the breeze, an animal, a stone, a scene—anything natural that attracts you.

4. Notice the pleasurable feeling this attraction provides you. Can you trust this feeling? Allow yourself to feel grateful for the pleasant feeling it provides.

5. Wait ten seconds, and notice whether you are still attracted and whether relating further to this attraction feels safe. If not, or if another attraction draws your attention, move on to a new attraction. You are seeking only Green/ Green experiences. *Do not proceed further if at any time you no longer feel safe or attracted.* Move on instead to something you do find safe and attractive.

6. Note how you feel physically and mentally now compared to how you felt before you started this activity. What value does this feeling have to you?

7. Given that it continues to feel safe and attractive, explore whatever has attracted you more fully. Experience it through as many senses as possible: sight, sound, touch, smell. Experience it with your eyes open and closed. Notice light, color, movement, location, and everything else you can about it, including the thoughts and feelings it engenders.

8. Now, as long as it feels safe, move closer until you sense it no longer feels attractive or safe to move any closer. If possible, begin to push against it. Notice when it resists and is no longer willing to move with your pressure.

9. Notice the relationship between this attraction and the rest of the natural environment around it. How does it fit? What does it contribute to? How is it supported? How does it respond to you? How do you fit there? How do you contribute? How are *you* supported by it?

CAROLYN'S EXPERIENCE WITH SENSORY REVALIDATION

Because Carolyn's days were already jammed packed with things she needed to monitor, she felt that Mental Monitoring would only add to the pressure she was feeling, so she chose to experiment with Sensory Revalidation. She was skeptical at first. She wasn't sure the activities could address her issues, and, given her busy schedule and urban location, she also doubted she would find the time or the natural places in which to do them.

She soon found, however, that her breaks were ideal times for doing the activities, and the yard behind the facility where she worked was more pleasant and natural than she had expected. She noticed birds, foliage, and a large overground rock she could sit on beside the patio. She later discovered there was also a small park just a few blocks away. After a while she began sharing the activities with her daughters occasionally, and they began exploring their own yard and neighborhood together.

"I was surprised at what I've learned from these activities," she reported. One day, for example, she was especially pressed at work. "I felt like there was no escaping from the difficulties of my life. I felt hounded." So, on her break she went out into the yard behind the facility and sat down on the rock beside the patio. "It was hot. The sun was beating down on me, and I felt all the more miserable. I shaded my eyes with my hands, but I couldn't escape the oppression of the sun. I felt as trapped by this sun as I did by my job, but then it suddenly dawned on me that I wasn't attracted to this spot at all today. So, why had I chosen to sit there?" The reason popped quickly into her mind, "It was handy. It was the first available spot."

"That's exactly what I do all the time," she wrote. "I settle for what's available, whatever is handiest." She quickly looked around for something that was actually attractive to her and headed for the grass under a tree in the far corner of the yard. "I felt like there was nothing I could do about the sun, just like I feel like there's nothing I can do about changing my life. But there was an attractive place right there waiting for me if I just looked a little further."

After several weeks, Carolyn reviewed her list of Warning Signals:

"Life seems to work against me."

"I know this is bad, but I can't imagine things being otherwise."

"Something always sabotages my best efforts."

"You can't trust anything that seems really good."

"As bad as it is, it's not that bad; I can take it."

"I've just got to put up with this."

"There's nothing I can do about it."

"Life is hard. There's always a lot you have to put up with."

"I have to do this. I don't have a choice."

"They all seem to be related to my not pursuing Green/Green feelings," she wrote. "My life was Green/Orange." Later when she reviewed the list, she realized she had already begun making different choices in her life. She had delegated many of the tasks at work that weren't Green/Green for her. She began standing up for herself with the administration at work. She wasn't willing, for example, to take on any more work without a raise or at least additional staff. And even though she said no, they didn't fire her. "How could they? They'd never find anyone who would do what I do for so little money!"

(continues)

(continued)

She knew this change was happening almost without her noticing it because in doing the activities every day, "I kept noticing how whether it was a branch or a stone or our cat, other things only let us go so far and then they resist."

Within a few months, Carolyn not only knew she could leave her job but realized she didn't want to consult with other eldercare facilities. "I had been taking care of older people since I was a child. It's a noble pursuit, but I never really chose it. It was just handy and familiar because of my taking care of my grandmother."

Six months later, Carolyn opened a licensed family day care program in her home. "I love working with the kids," she reported. "Yes, I'm still taking care of others, and I'm not making as much money as I would have by consulting, but the happiest time in my life was when I was at home when my daughters were young. These kids give me so much joy. I get far more than I give, including more money than I was making. It works out because I can hold my ground now. I don't let the parents take advantage of me. I couldn't have done that before.

"I had to take a stand with my daughters, too. They were put out at first about having a bunch of little kids around the house. They had a million complaints, but I didn't fold. We sat down and arranged our house so we could each have our own space. Now, they even like earning extra money by helping me out in my business. My life feels very Green/Green these days."

10. When it no longer feels attractive to continue this exercise, note that this attraction and its environment have supported and cooperated in enabling you to do this activity, and, if it feels reasonable, express your appreciation.

11. In your journal, describe what you experienced, and list the three most important things you learned from doing this activity that day.

12. If it feels attractive, share this experience with someone else.

Weekly Activity

Once a week, look back at the hang-up you identified at the beginning of your journal. Review the reactions you checked off under it. Do they still apply to you? Look again at the list of Warning Signals and RX Summary. Reflect on any changes you've noticed in your reactions. Is anything you've been experiencing or learning from the daily activities relevant to the role these reactions and issues play in your life? Write your reflections in your journal.

When the initial hang-up you identified is no longer an issue, select another hang-up, if you have one; write it in your journal; and continue your daily exercises.

Many people find Sensory Revalidation a more enjoyable way to reprogram mental hang-ups. They enjoy the activities and love the freedom of not concentrating on their problems. They like the way the activities result in positive changes almost without effort and certainly without having to monitor themselves. They feel it's a more spontaneous and natural way to reset their mental programming.

Because Sensory Revalidation is quite different from the models for change that are popular in our culture, others find it to be a foreign way to learn and change. They're uncomfortable with not knowing exactly what's happening and don't feel it enables them to stay in control by consciously monitoring and directing the changes they're making.

If you find this method appealing yet feel at a loss in doing it on your own, or if you would like to learn a wealth of additional

Sensory Revalidation activities, you may want to participate in an online class on applied ecopsychology (such classes start continually through www.JustAskaTree.com).

From the issues and information in this chapter, identify three things you want or need to do. Write them down in the Personal Action Plan in Appendix A: Take-Off Section, beginning on page 294.

CHAPTER EIGHT

But My Problems Are Real!

How can I become my own boss with a disability?

What if my friends and family are against me?

How can I get people to take me seriously?

What am I going to do if I lose my health insurance?

Maybe you have a disability and are unable to walk or type on a keyboard. Maybe you're a single mother who is already working a 24/7 schedule, between a regular job and taking care of a demanding family. Maybe you never graduated from high school, or your friends and family not only do not support your ideas of self-employment but actively oppose them.

In short, in addition to the normal challenges of starting a business, you have problems that make it harder for you to achieve your dreams of self-employment and independence. In answering the following questions, this chapter will demonstrate that even the most serious problems—problems that most people can barely imagine, much less experience—can be overcome, that becoming your own boss is within your reach:

1. What if I have physical incapabilities or disabilities?
2. What if I'm too young or too old or a single mom or a dropout or . . . ?
3. How can I get more support from friends and family?
4. What if I lose my health insurance and other benefits?

Question 1: What If I Have Physical Incapabilities or Disabilities?

Working for someone else—in a regular, full-time job or career—can be a difficult proposition at best for someone with a disability, even in these days of the Americans with Disabilities Act (which requires employers to make certain accommodations at work to avoid shutting people with disabilities out of the workforce). If you need a wheelchair to get around, for example, riding the subway back and forth to the office each day will be an exercise in extreme patience and perseverance. If you cannot hear or see, standard office tools such as telephones and computers may be difficult or impossible to use without special modifications. If you have a chronic illness that saps your energy or subjects you to frequent bouts of nausea or seizures, maintaining a regular work schedule may be nearly impossible.

Indeed, if you are faced with problems like these, it might be easier simply to forget about working altogether. But many, many people with disabilities and other physical incapabilities have found great satisfaction—and financial rewards—in having jobs and careers, and a very large number have also found that being self-employed actually offers the best of both worlds. Not only can you make good money with your own business but, since you're the boss, you can come and go as you please, working around your own schedules and deciding when and where you will work.

Would it surprise you to learn that people with disabilities in the United States have a higher rate of self-employment and small business experience than people without disabilities? It's true. According to the 1990 U.S. Census, 12.2 percent of people with disabilities are either self-employed or have small business experience, while only 7.8 percent of people without disabilities are self-employed or have small business experience.

Why is self-employment such an attractive option for people with disabilities? Here are some of the key reasons:

> People with disabilities in the United States have a higher rate of self-employment and small business experience than people without disabilities.

- You can be truly independent.
- You can work at home if you like.
- You can implement your own accessible and supportive work environment.
- You can tailor your work schedule to your personal or medical needs, arriving, leaving, and taking breaks whenever you like.
- You don't have to rely on anyone else to get you to work.
- You can still qualify for Social Security or Supplemental Security payments so long as you stay within certain income limits.

For people with disabilities—just as for people without disabilities—self-employment can be your key to your dream of independence. Regardless of these advantages of self-employment for people with disabilities, a number of very real obstacles often confront hopeful entrepreneurs with disabilities. These potential obstacles include the following:

- A general lack of information on how to start a business tailored to the needs of people with disabilities
- Difficulty in raising capital
- Small business development programs rarely targeting people with disabilities
- Few programs for people with disabilities (rehab, life skills, etc.) that encourage entrepreneurship
- Potential loss of Social Security or Supplemental Security disability programs (if income from self-employment exceeds certain limits)
- Potential loss of health care, housing, and other benefits and subsidies
- Discrimination

Although these obstacles may be formidable, they can be overcome. Every day, people with disabilities—in all kinds of businesses—have been able to turn their dreams of self-employment into reality. And so can you.

Ryan Peralta of St. Clair Shores, Michigan, was born with quadrimembral limb deficiency, which left him without any functional arms or legs. Twenty-two years later, Ryan—whose physical disabilities would make it difficult for him to find a regular job with any conventional business—found that there was a way to sidestep the issue altogether: by starting his own business. Ryan is founder of NewMedia3, a successful Web design and graphic arts business that has landed many Detroit-area businesses as clients. He says, "Web design isn't about the way you write [computer code]; it's about a Web site's look and feel, and for me that's an art form."

The proliferation of computers and the explosion of the Internet has created enormous opportunities for people with severe disabilities to start their own business and to achieve their dreams of independence. Says Kenny Rudolph, president and

---

SUCCESS AFTER TRAGEDY

When Heidi Van Arnem was seventeen, she was accidentally shot in the neck by a friend's brother, instantly paralyzing her from the neck down and leaving her arms with only limited use. Until her recent death from respiratory failure, however, Heidi refused to let her disability get in the way of her dreams of independence, first starting and running a successful travel agency, and then starting iCan! Inc.—a solutions and services company for people with disabilities and leaders of business—and iCan.com. The key to her success? Computers and the Internet revolution. Referring to her laptop computer, Heidi said, "With this, I'm just as productive as the next person. Without it, I need someone to open the drawer for me and take out a piece of paper."

---

chief operating officer of online disabilities organization iCan! Inc., "In a lot of cases, the Internet is allowing people with severe disabilities—who clearly have significant barriers to employment—to work from their homes. There's no question the Internet and technology have created more employment opportunities for people with disabilities. It's bridging the divide between people with disabilities and the general population."

In the case of Gayle Van Dam, a Web entrepreneur with multiple sclerosis, the Internet has allowed her to reach a diverse and international audience for her unique walking sticks, plungers, and umbrellas made with tassels, antique doorknobs, and leather through her www.classycanes.com Web site. According to Gayle, "The Internet is an incredible way to communicate and get out of the house, get out of the chair, and run a business. It's opened up a whole new world for people with disabilities."

Of course, people with disabilities can and do start all kinds of businesses, some using computers and the Internet, and others not. Here are several examples of people with disabilities who refused to let their very real problems stand in the way of achieving their dreams of success:

- After suffering a stroke that left him with limited movement in his arm and hand, master sign maker Ed Terranova of Kettering, Ohio, was referred to a self-employment program. While in this program, Ed created a business plan for a computer-based design firm—a plan that he put into effect soon afterward. Nova Sign & Design's success required Ed to move his business out of his home and into a nearby commercial space that will allow for plenty of growth. Ed Terranova's goal? To train and hire people with disabilities to work in his business, thereby helping others help themselves.

- After an accident left her unable to walk, Lesley Ross—who had formerly worked as a food and beverage manager for a country club in South Africa, and as a personal assistant to several different executives—decided to start her own business. After researching her options, Lesley decided on starting a virtual office services company. But, before she could start her company—which she named Our Other Office—Lesley had to finish months of hospital stays and physiotherapy. By the time she was ready to start, she had burned through most of her savings, meaning she would have to be very frugal in launching her business. Lesley built a Web site, printed 2,500 flyers, and sent out a flood of e-mail messages to advertise her business. Through hard work and perseverance, Lesley turned her business into a successful enterprise. Her advice to others? "Keep your mind focused on the road ahead and aim for it. Talk to people, and never stop asking for help and advice. One day your dream will become a reality, and you will wake up each morning like I do, ready to enjoy your day because when you are doing something you love, it is not a job but an enjoyable and rewarding life."

- Motivated by an automobile accident that left him paraplegic, Joseph Jarke invented a wheelchair for people with disabilities whose jobs require them to travel frequently. Airline aisles are often too narrow for a standard wheelchair to fit. Joseph's innovation was a compact wheelchair that folds into a package about the size of a briefcase. Joseph started a company to sell his invention—SeatCase, Inc.—to enthusiastic airlines looking for alternatives to unwieldy and hard-to-stow traditional wheelchairs. Says Joseph, "We really have changed the world in a small way."

- Russell Jennings founded Nomad Art Glass in Columbus, Ohio, after contracting Guillain-Barré syndrome, a disease that left the muscles in his upper body severely weakened. Through this home-based business, Russell creates, markets, and sells a variety of three-dimensional window hangings, Tiffany-style lamps, door panels, and more for local individuals and businesses, including a local cocktail lounge, which bought five lampshades. Word-of-mouth advertising is growing, and Nomad Art Glass didn't take long to show a profit.

- Michael David Aronin—who has cerebral palsy—decided to quit his job placing workers with disabilities for the state of Maryland and start his own home-based business, Rising Above, in Odenton, Maryland. Under the auspices of his company, Michael offers inspirational speaking services—mixed with a bit of humor—to professional and business groups. He thought of the idea for his business when he was performing in comedy clubs in the early

1990s. According to Michael, "Several times during my career on stage, people have come up after my shows and said, 'Not only did you make us laugh, but you inspired me and I learned a lot tonight.' From that, I knew I was on to something, and I started to research how to become a speaker and moved into addressing businesses at luncheons and conferences."

- After losing his sight when he was twenty-nine years old, James Stovall launched the Narrative Television Network (NTN) in Tulsa, Oklahoma. NTN produces specially modified soundtracks for films and television shows, targeted to blind and vision-impaired people. The soundtracks add voice-overs describing the actual settings and other visual elements of these films and television shows, so that the "viewers" can create their own images in their minds. Despite the efforts of many technical experts to dissuade him from this effort, James persisted, eventually building a network with annual revenues of more than $6 million and a reach of more than twenty-five million homes around the world.

KEY RESOURCES

If you have a disability and are interested in starting your own business, here are some terrific resources to check out first:

- U.S. Department of Labor, Office of Disability Employment Policy: www.dol.gov/odep
- iCan.com: www.ican.com
- The S.E.E.D. Institute: http://remote-ability.com/seed/seed.html
- National Organization on Disability: www.nod.org

From reading these stories, what are some of the qualities of the successful small business owner who has a disability? According to iCan.com, they are the same qualities that bring nondisabled small business owners success. Here are some of these qualities:

Self-starter

Loves his or her work

Total commitment and belief in his or her product or service

Willing to sacrifice in the short term for long-term success

Knows the competition better than anyone

Determines the marketing niche of the product or service

Leads by example in work ethic, time management, honesty, and integrity

Maintains a balance of family life, work, and play

Persistence

So, no matter what real problems you face, if you're motivated strongly enough by your dreams of independence and self-employment, there's really nothing that can stop you from achieving your goals. Time and time again, people with even the most severe disabilities and physical inabilities have proven that to be the case, and so can you.

You don't have to put your dreams on hold; make it happen!

Question 2: What If I'm Too Young or Too Old or a Single Mom or a Dropout or . . . ?

Almost anything can become an obstacle in your pathway to independence if you allow it to. Have you ever heard anyone

Reaping a Harvest at the S.E.E.D. Institute

Andy Leaf and Julie Damon founded the S.E.E.D. Institute in Costa Mesa, California, in 1995. At the time, Andy (who is quadriplegic) and Julie (who is legally blind) felt there were no opportunities for people with disabilities to better learn how to start and run a business. Says Andy, "The quality of instruction in the junior college system was pretty bad. The SBA library was antiquated—they had one computer, and it was broken—and it was very poorly organized. So we thought, maybe there were other people like ourselves who had similar problems who would like to be independent. We had our first seminar at Irvine Valley College in 1995, and it was a sell-out. We were amazed that there were that many people who wanted to come. So, we thought if there were that many people, we should put together a nonprofit. A couple of years after that, we developed our programs, put on seminars, and published a newsletter."

The S.E.E.D. Institute offers complete programs in starting and running a small business, tailored to the specific needs of people with disabilities. According to Andy, "People come to us with their ideas; we help them develop them. We help with their market research to see if it's a viable business in the marketplace, and we help them develop their business plan. About 120 students have gone through our program—it takes about sixty hours of staff and student time to put together a good business plan. There's a lot of hands-on with our students." Of this group of students, approximately 47 percent are still running their own small

(perhaps yourself?) use one or more of the following excuses for not following up on an opportunity?

"I'm a single parent—I don't have time to take on anything else in my life."

businesses in the Los Angeles and Orange County areas, while the majority of the rest are still awaiting funding to finance their start-ups.

A wide variety of people with disabilities—and a wide variety of different business ideas—have found their way to the S.E.E.D. Institute. According to Andy, "We had one guy with chronic pain—couldn't sit for more than fifteen minutes at a time—who started a computer repair business. He couldn't work in a regular office environment, but now he can work at his own pace. He's doing quite well. There's one guy we helped who invented a heart valve. Another guy who has a high-performance auto parts business—he's blind—and he's doing very well. And we helped a blind photographer. He was a photographer when he became ill; the medication he took caused him to become legally blind. He can no longer do high-fashion photography, but now he's doing shots of pets and their owners."

The instructors at S.E.E.D. make no illusions about the challenges that students will face when starting their own businesses. Says Andy, "Our coursework is really difficult, and we make our students work very hard. We make it clear that this is not something that's going to be easy—you're going to have to work at it. If you want it, then that's great. A lot of our students come in already motivated because they've always had an idea that they wanted to do something; we've showed them opportunities to do that."

"I'm too young—no one will take me seriously."

"I'm too old—my better days are behind me."

"I dropped out of school—I'll never amount to much."

"I'm African American [or Asian American, Latino, female, gay, lesbian, or any other discriminated-against group]— I can't catch a break."

"I've had a hard life—how can I get beyond my past?"

The fact is, no matter what kinds of problems or obstacles are in your path, you can overcome them. For every problem you've got, thousands of people with the same problem have achieved their own goals of self-employment and independence. Believe in yourself—and in your own abilities—and you will do the same.

> For every problem you've got, thousands of people with the same problem have achieved their own goals of self-employment and independence.

In the stories that follow, you'll see how a variety of people overcame their own problems to find success in starting their own businesses. Some thought they were too young to be successful; some thought they were too old. Some were discriminated against because they were black, gay, or women. Some were single parents or stay-at-home moms. Some had serious illnesses, and some had addictions to drugs or alcohol. Some were dropouts, and some were abused by their spouses or their parents. All had serious obstacles in their lives that a belief in themselves, strength of character, and no small amount of perseverance allowed them to overcome.

I'M TOO OLD, OR I'M TOO YOUNG . . .

Recouping the Nest Egg

Bill and Lanie Isgrig—sixty-five and fifty-one years old, respectively—were semiretired and living in Las Vegas when the dot-com bubble burst, taking much of their retirement nest egg along with it. "We lost a lot, and we thought, 'What are we going to do to recoup?'" Bill and Lanie could have returned to the corporate world where they came from, but both had already had their fill of that scene. Instead, they merged their expertise and backgrounds to start their own company—Rim Solutions, a document management and storage company. "We locked ourselves in our home, pounded out a business plan, and took it to a local bank. They took one look and said, 'Come on in, we'll give you some money.' We put up $27,000; they put up $63,000."

Although Bill and Lanie are routinely working ten- or twelve-hour days, they love it. And, they're making good money doing what they want to do. "We're doing exactly what we wanted to do. Our reason for doing it was ambiguous, but now that we've done it, we're really happy."

A Ten-Year-Old Entrepreneur

Kathryn Gregory of Bedford, Massachusetts, was only ten years old when she came up with the idea for a new invention. While building a snow fort with her brother, Kathryn became frustrated when she couldn't stop snow from working its way up the sleeves of her winter coat. Along with her mother, Kathryn designed a synthetic fleece cylinder that would provide a barrier between sleeves and gloves, keeping snow out. After testing and refining the design, Kathryn gave prototypes out to the members of her Girl Scout troop, where it was judged a winner. Kathryn trademarked a name for her invention—Wristies—applied for a patent, and started a company, Wristies, Inc. A few years ago, Kathryn became the youngest person ever to sell on cable television marketplace QVC (earning $22,000 in sales in just six minutes), and she has signed purchasing agreements with McDonald's, FedEx, and the Girl Scouts.

Key Questions: *The age that you project to others is much more a function of how young (or old) you feel inside than it is tied to a calendar or clock. Does your dream of independence make you feel so excited that you're energized to make it happen? Is it inspiring enough to push you past the naysayers who stand in your way? If not, what would it take to make it so?*

But I Am Physically Not Well . . .

A Sensational Recovery

Suzanne Locklear's dream was to create and sell a yummy new salad dressing that she had developed. There was only one problem standing in the way of this Boise, Idaho, native: She had just been diagnosed with breast cancer. And not for the first time, but for the second. But pulled by a real desire to start her own business—and pushed by the tenuousness of her own mortality—Suzanne resolved to start a business that would allow her to sell her product, while promoting cancer awareness and a healthy lifestyle. Says Suzanne, "I want people to know that cancer is not a death sentence. Cancer made me a lot bolder and braver because I figured, 'What do I have to lose?'"

With the help of her family and friends, Suzanne started bottling her dressing in her own kitchen and selling it in specialty stores and via mail order under the name of her company, Suzanne's Sensationals, while committing to donating a portion of her proceeds to breast cancer research. Suzanne sold two hundred twelve-bottle cases of dressing in her first year in business; today her products can be found in more than 1,300 stores in the western United States. Suzanne's Web site (www.suzannesfoods.com) is chock-full of information and links on breast cancer, as well as recipes and a complete presentation of her company's products.

Suzanne sums up her experience by saying, "Building this business has many twists and turns. The message is that it's important for all women to take care of their loved ones by first taking care of themselves."

Two Businesses, One Illness

Carol Dick founded her first business—Heart 'N Home—to produce and sell handcrafted items such as candleholders from her home in Port Elgin, Ontario. She grew the business from selling just a few items at local craft fairs to stocking an inventory of more than one hundred different items sold through a Canadian craft store chain, consignment shops, and artist shows. Jumping onto the e-commerce bandwagon, she soon created a Web site to market and wholesale her products directly to gift shops around the world. Unfortunately, a devastating illness required Carol to shut down her business in 1999. Says Carol, "It was the hardest choice I have ever had to make, but I am a true believer that everything happens for a reason. I made this my mantra for the next year while I focused all my energies on getting well again."

Carol did steadily get better, and she soon felt the draw of self-employment once again. But this time, she had a different plan. "My health improved steadily, and I eventually began to think about working again. I knew I couldn't resume my woodworking business, and I felt lost when comparing all the online possibilities. Most opportunities I came across just didn't seem to suit or inspire me, and many of the ones that did weren't available to Canadians." As time went on, however, friends, family, and other acquaintances began asking Carol for computer advice, and she was happy to share what she knew, eventually designing and building Web sites for many of them. She had found her calling: to start a new Web site design business.

According to Carol, "Everything seemed to just click, and my new business, The Web Nook, was launched. I realized I hadn't previously run into a roadblock at all, just a fork in the road, and I had found my way again." Her advice to others? "Know your priorities, follow your heart, believe in yourself, and trust that everything happens for a reason."

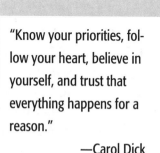

"Know your priorities, follow your heart, believe in yourself, and trust that everything happens for a reason."

—Carol Dick

Key Questions: Serious illness can take the wind out of anyone's sails. While you'll be hard-pressed to start a business if you're lying in a hospital bed with tubes hanging out of your arms and a respirator stuck in your throat, as long as your brain is working, you can plan and set goals that will help you make your dream reality. What can you do today to get you closer to your dream? What can you do tomorrow, and the day after that, and the day after that?

I DROPPED OUT OF SCHOOL . . .

Junking College for a Fortune

College dropout Brian Scudamore started his business—Rubbish Boys Disposal Service, Inc., a junk removal business in Vancouver, British Columbia—with an old pickup truck and a cash stake of $700. It specializes in hauling away the things that are too large for local trash collectors, too junky for the Salvation Army, and too small for name-brand industrial waste companies. Today, Brian's business, since renamed

1-800-Got-Junk?, has grown to more than thirty-six franchises across the United States and Canada, bringing in more than $12 million in annual revenues.

Early on, Brian knew that the business had growth potential; he just didn't know how huge. He says, "I realized we had the potential to be bigger than the two trucks we had. I didn't have the vision that we'd be a national company; I just hoped to be big in Vancouver." Indeed, the company has grown exponentially since its founding, hauling more than eighty thousand truckloads of junk at between $300 and $400 a truckload. While a typical customer asks the company to haul away old sofas and broken appliances, some of the more interesting loads include nineteen thousand expired cans of sardines, two truckloads of snail shells (from a bankrupt escargot importer), and an empty coffin.

Says Brian, "My dad said to me, 'You're dropping out of school to be a junk man?!' He jokes about it today and is blown away by what it's become."

Whiz Kid

Like Bill Gates before him—who famously dropped out of Harvard to found a small business, Microsoft, with friend Paul Allen—Jayson Meyer dropped out of school (high school, in Jayson's case) to start up his own customized computer hardware and software development business, Meyer Technologies, Inc., of Daytona Beach, Florida. The spark came when he was riding home from school one day in his father's car: "Why not just start a company, call it Meyer Technologies, and see where it goes?"

Using $1,500 that he had saved from mowing lawns and repairing computers for friends and neighbors, he started his business out of a booth at a local flea market. Today, Jayson works eighty- to hundred-hour weeks, and his revenues have grown from $4,000 its first year to more than $1.5 million today—more than enough business to afford a brand-new silver Lexus automobile and a Rolex watch. While Jayson has already found great success, he is convinced that he has mined only the tip of the iceberg thus far. He says, "I think there's global potential for any young company that offers better computer systems and service."

Key Questions: For some period of time, almost everyone assumed that, to be successful, you had to graduate from high school or college. Countless entrepreneurs have proven that definitely not to be the case. If you're a dropout, are you using that as an excuse to put your dreams of independence and self-employment on hold? What would you really like to do with your life? What would you do if you could quit your current job and work for yourself? Why not start that exact business while you keep your day job?

SOME PEOPLE DON'T LIKE THE WAY I AM . . .

Creating Compassion

Greg Nimer is gay, and he started his Hollywood, California–based greeting card business—10% Productions, which is mostly targeted to gays and lesbians—after his controversial designs were rejected by mainstream greeting card publishers. Greg's greeting cards cover most of the same topics as do the ones you'll find at your local Hallmark shop—love, unions, birthdays, anniversaries, friendship, sympathy, and more—but with a twist. But while some cards targeted to the gay and lesbian communities often tend to be rated somewhere north of PG-13, Greg is proud that his cards are fairly tame in comparison. He says, "We're homo-Hallmark. We're safe in comparison to other companies."

As safe as his cards may be, Nimer's business is no stranger to the risky side effects of discrimination against gays and lesbians. "When we first started, we were getting death threats," says Greg. "Mall associations were telling retailers carrying our cards to stop or leave." So how's business today? Very good, thank you. According to Greg, his products have been quickly embraced by the gay and lesbian communities, and they are making slow-but-steady inroads into mainline stores—selling in numbers that Nimer will only say amounts to "millions" of dollars worth a year. And, as acceptance of gays and lesbians continues to grow, this success can only continue. As 10% Production's mission statement says in part, "We believe in a world of love, compassion, and mutual respect, a world free from fear, discrimination, and prejudice." This is a goal that inspired Greg Nimer to start his business, and it continues to inspire him every day.

A Toast to Women Entrepreneurs

Veronica Pekarovic is a woman who has created a very successful business of her own in an industry traditionally dominated by men—importing and selling her own brand of flavored vodka named Zone Vodka. Veronica started her business—R&A Imports—out of her home in Pacific Palisades, California, after selling her telecommunications company and ending up with a nice profit. To create a unique product, Veronica paired a low-alcohol version of Italian-distilled wheat vodka (only 50 proof, versus 80 proof for most vodka) with trendy fruit flavors. Says Veronica, "As a mother, I feel a sense of responsibility. Someone can comfortably drink a glass of Zone, and they're okay." The vodka comes in a unique, slim, frosted glass bottle and in five natural fruit flavors: banana, peach, melon, tangerine, and lemon. Interestingly enough, men and women prefer different flavors. According to Veronica, "Women tend toward peach and melon, and the men tend toward banana and tangerine."

While Zone is making inroads into the national liquor industry—it has been featured at many celebrity events, including post-Oscar parties and other Hollywood happenings—the journey hasn't been easy for this woman in a man's world. Says Veronica, "I think there is something masculine about liquor and the perception of liquor. There are one or two other women in the country who own their own brands. But if you were to ask me would I do it all over again, I'd say yes."

Key Questions: Sadly, discrimination is still very much a part of the human condition, and it takes a particular brand of fortitude to overcome its effects. If you've been discriminated against, what can you personally do to get beyond it? How can you step around this problem and find the path to your dreams? Do you need to adopt a new attitude, find a new location, or start a different kind of business? Or serve the very group you're part of?

But It's Hard Being a Mom . . .

An Answered Prayer

More than thirty years ago, single mom Edna Perry of Kansas City, Missouri, prayed for a way to make more money for her three children. Working as a secretary, she couldn't bear the thought that her children would be condemned to the poverty that she herself had faced as the eldest of fifteen children of a Baptist deacon, and she put her faith in God to help her find an answer. According to Edna, that answer came in the form of a dream in which God told her to become a real estate broker and to be her own boss. Edna started her new business— Edna E. Perry Real Estate Co.—shortly thereafter, with $50 in savings and a borrowed typewriter, and sold her first house within a week. Today, specializing in relocating churches and synagogues to new places of worship—and helping low-income families find homes of their own—Edna has built a successful enterprise with her own two hands.

Despite her success, Edna still remembers where she came from. "I learned how to work hard," she says. "When you don't have much and you're from a big family, you appreciate what you have later on." Edna is particularly interested in helping young women get into the real estate business, and she appreciates the impact that she can have on others. She says, "Some young women don't think they can accomplish things. It helps to have someone let them know they can do it."

Managing the Home Front

Soon after starting her business—Office Angel, a typing service in Taupo, New Zealand—in an office space in town, Donna Tindle realized that her sales weren't sufficient to pay the rent. Her decision? To move her business into her home. As a single mother of a three-year-old boy, this change not only has significantly reduced her business expenses but has also allowed her to spend more time with her son. To be more responsive to her clients, Donna set up a delivery service to pick up and deliver their work product.

Donna has faced the inevitable challenges that every entrepreneur faces—she had to get out of her office lease, and she had early difficulties with a partner that needed to be resolved (the partnership was dissolved). But despite all that, Donna is extremely happy to have her own business and to be able to take care of both her business and her child at home.

Key Questions: Both single and married moms face special challenges, especially when they add starting their own business to their long list of domestic duties. If you're a busy mom,

---

OTHER INSPIRING PARENTS

Paul and Sarah Edwards and Lisa M. Roberts have 111 stories of moms and dads who have made a business and a life in their book *The Entrepreneurial Parent: How to Earn Your Living from Home and Still Enjoy Your Family, Your Work and Your Life* (Tarcher, 2002).

---

how can you make more time in your life to start your own business? Do you have friends or relatives who you can partner with, or who can help you watch your kids while you work on your business? Can you partner with your spouse or significant other, or can he take on a greater share of your domestic responsibilities?

I'VE HAD A REALLY HARD LIFE . . .

Rags to Riches

Bernice Richard's mother had a nervous breakdown when Bernice was eight years old, forcing Bernice to step into her mother's shoes, cooking, cleaning, and taking care of her younger brother and sister. At age nineteen, Bernice married and was a dutiful wife while her husband served in the military for ten years. But her husband tried to kill her, and Bernice divorced him, taking her two children back to her hometown to try to pick up the pieces of their shattered lives.

Hoping to rebuild her life, Bernice went on welfare and started doing all her clothes shopping at thrift stores and church fairs. Little did she know that her shopping would lead her to her own business opportunity.

Says Bernice, "It was my hobby . . . which was great therapy for me. I collected and restored the clothes I found. Then one day my neighbor said to me, 'You look wonderful in vintage clothing.' I was so insulted that she had noticed I was wearing old women's clothes. However, the words 'vintage clothing' rang in my ears." Bernice began to research the topic of vintage clothing, reading everything about it that she could get her hands on. Soon, she was an expert.

Remarried, Bernice says her new husband encouraged her to start her own vintage clothing boutique. She approached the SBA for advice and received free small business counseling through her local chamber of commerce. When a prospective business partner suggested they combine their resources, Bernice jumped at the opportunity. She says, "One day a woman called me. To this day I do not know how she found me. However, we started a venture together in an antique co-op shop we shared. She did antiques and I did clothing. I took my collection and a collection I purchased with my car insurance money (set aside and due six months later, $350) and restored the lovely garments I'd purchased. I then put eighteen of the forty restored pieces on a ten-foot wall and sold all eighteen for $1,000. Thus began my adventure of turning my hobby into a business. I went from $1,000 a month to up to $5,000 a month."

Today, Bernice Richard owns and operates her successful business—Reflections in Vintage Clothing—in Gardner, Massachusetts, and she gives back to her community, contributing her time to help other victims of domestic violence.

She Fought the Law—and Won

After catching her teenage son smoking marijuana one weekend—and spending $120 for a drug test at her local hospital emergency room—Sunny Cloud decided that there had to be a better way. Her goal: to create and market an affordable, at-home drug test. Within six months, Sunny had developed

Parent's Alert. With the kit—which costs only $45—parents can test their children for a variety of drugs, including opiates, marijuana, cocaine, PCP, benzodiazepines, and even alcohol (for an additional $15 charge).

After Sunny had sold about a thousand of her kits, the U.S. Food and Drug Administration (FDA) slapped her with a warning letter accusing her Atlanta-based company of distributing a misbranded and adulterated Class III medical device (which consisted of a plastic cup and jar—items that separately were already FDA approved—and a mailing label to a licensed lab). To say that Sunny was shocked to receive the letter would be an understatement. "If we're supposed to be legally responsible for our children's behavior, we need the tools," she says. "It's not a matter of whether you like the test, but a matter of whether you should have a choice to use the test."

Sunny hired a high-powered attorney who immediately challenged the FDA's determination and began to rally political leaders and the public to Sunny's cause. As public outrage boiled over, the FDA backed off, and the drug tests were given the green light. In a statement in support of Sunny and Parent's Alert, House Commerce Committee chairman Tom Bliley said, "Sunny Cloud stood up to the entire federal government—and the government backed down. As a result, thousands of American kids and their parents will have the best tool they could ever get to 'just say no'—a simple, easy-to-use test for drugs that can be used in complete confidence. On behalf of the people I represent here in Washington, I want to thank her."

Key Questions: It's easy to become distracted from your goals when you've had to fight every inch of the way to make your dreams reality. Remember, however, that the past is the past, and you make your own future. What can you do to start living in the here and now, and to move beyond the challenges that once beset you? How can you turn the lessons you've learned into action? What can you do right now to move forward toward achieving your goals?

Question 3: How Can I Get More Support from Friends and Family?

No man, or woman, is an island. Relationships impact us every day and in every way. Family, friends, neighbors, spouses, significant others, and colleagues provide love, challenges, and company. If we're blessed, our relationships support us but do something else as well. When our relationships are supportive, they provide us with an extra boost that can help us overcome the inevitable obstacles in the path to our dreams. But, when our relationships are negative and take away from us and what we want to become, then they themselves become blockages that we must overcome before we can achieve our goals. Consciously or not, those we count on act as friendly saboteurs.

When Rob Steir, founder and CEO of MBAGlobalNet .com, decided to leave his career position in the commercial real estate industry, he had the support of his parents, but he did not have the support of his girl-

> When our relationships are supportive, they provide us with an extra boost that can help us overcome the inevitable obstacles in the path to our dreams.

friend. Says Rob, "My family was very supportive of it. My dad ran his own pharmacy for thirty years. When you're coming from a small business environment, the freedom of being your own boss coupled with corporate America—where you're not your own boss, and you have to be at the whim of someone else's political decisions—you start to see clearly: 'Hey, I want to do this.'

"On the other hand, I had a girlfriend for three years, and she was not very supportive of my business idea—it all revolved around money and financial stability. She asked me to choose: my dream or her. I chose my dream, and we're no longer involved."

The problem comes down to this: Most people are not big fans of change. And people who are not big fans of change don't want those around them to change, either. They resist it—in themselves and in others. But when the people you rely on for support actively sabotage your dreams and become obstacles in the path of achieving your dreams, then you've got a real problem.

Do any of these common sabotage tactics sound familiar?

Withdrawing from you and putting less energy into your relationship

Criticizing you and your plans for independence

Becoming overly involved in your life and trying to redirect your efforts

How can you get more support from the people who are important in your life? Here are some tips for getting the support you need and keeping yourself on the path to achieving your dreams of independence:

- *Identify your true friends and foes.* If you're like most of us, you've got lots of family, friends, business associates, and others who spend time with you. But, as you probably know, just because you spend a lot of time with someone, that doesn't mean that he or she really supports you and your efforts toward independence. Before you can get more support from those who mean the most to you, you've got to first figure out who's on your side and who's not. Take a close look at each of your acquaintances—who supports you, and who tries to undermine you or sabotage your efforts? Don't just trust your own gut; get the opinion of your most trusted friends and relatives.

- *Understand what you can change (and what you cannot change).* Remember that you cannot change the way other people feel; you can only change the way that you feel. While you may be able to influence the thinking of important people in your life—perhaps eventually leading them to change their thinking—you cannot count on them to change just because you want them to.

- *Ignore those who are not supportive of your dreams.* You can't expect everyone else to buy into your dreams of success and independence. In fact, you can expect some of your friends and family to try actively to dissuade you from pursuing them. The best thing you can do is be polite but refuse to allow someone else's priorities or concerns to take precedence over your own.

    According to Renee Walkup, founder and president of SalesPEAK, Inc., a sales training firm in Atlanta, Georgia, "When I began my business, someone said I was crazy to quit my high-paying position to start a company. I heard every negative story you can imagine. I put on a happy face and stuck to my work. Sometimes people throw negativity at you because they have their own agenda."

- *Spend more time with your true friends and less time with your foes.* If you allow others—loved ones or not—to sabotage your dreams of independence, then you really have no one to blame but yourself for allowing it to happen. As soon as you identify the people who are working actively against the change that you represent, put them at the bottom of your list of people to see and things to do. As soon as you identify the people who are your true friends and supporters, put them at the very top of your list. In other words, focus your time and energy on your most supportive relationships, and spend as little time and energy as possible on relationships with people who are working against you.

- *Create new networks of supporters.* Although we all hope that our friends and loved ones will support us when we decide to leave the security of a career to start our own business, that is often not the case. The solution? Create new networks of supporters, particularly people who are already doing what you want to do. Says small business owner Barbara Winter, "Although I didn't realize it at first, my early business days would have been happier if I knew a few other women entrepreneurs. It wasn't until my second year in business that I met some women who were also building their own businesses. Those relationships became powerful, positive forces in my life." No doubt they helped Barbara reinforce the fact that she had made the right decision in starting her own business.

- *Let your supporters know what you need.* If you need help, ask for it. If you need support, be sure your supporters know what you're looking for. If you need resources, don't be shy—figure out exactly what you need, and then go to your supporters to find them. If anyone is ready to help, it's your supporters—give them a chance to show you how much they care.

- *Keep moving forward.* So long as you keep moving forward, you'll be able to deal with—and step around—the people in your life who would prefer to have you stay the way you've always been, instead of watching you reach for your dreams.

Says Barry Farber, president of Farber Training Systems in Livingston, New Jersey, "I make a massive amount of calls. Once I dive in and start seeing a little progress, my whole attitude starts to turn around because I know small progress eventually becomes big business. That keeps me going. Everything starts with that first little step."

When you're getting ready to start your new business, having supporters can be a very real asset, and their power to help you make your business happen cannot be underestimated. Before you take another step, figure out who's on your side—and who's not—and then do what you need to do to increase the positive energy in your relationships while decreasing the negative.

> Figure out who's on your side—and who's not—and then do what you need to do to increase the positive energy in your relationships while decreasing the negative.

Key Questions: Who are the people standing between you and your dreams of independence? Why have they decided to hinder you rather than help you? Can you put those people aside while you take time to identify your true supporters, or can you reach out to meet an entirely new group of supporters? Where can you find like-minded people who have gone through the same thing you're going through? Where can you meet people who have already done what you want to do?

Question 4: What If I Lose My Health Insurance and Other Benefits?

One of the biggest concerns for people thinking about starting their own business is that they will lose the benefits that their full-time job or career provides them with. Indeed, for those of you who live in the United States, we're in the middle of a health care crisis. It is extremely difficult for self-employed individuals to find health care coverage that is both comprehensive and affordable.

When Pat Canary, today the owner of AlphaGraphics, a small quick-printing service located in Vernon Hills, Illinois, worked for big businesses such as Deloitte & Touche and a large, international transportation company, he took health care benefits for granted. Today, however, after his business was rocked by skyrocketing premiums, he has had to dig hard to find the best deals for his employees and himself. Pat sums it all up with four simple words: "It has gone crazy."

Sammy Davis Jr., owner of Handyman at Work, a small home and business repair and maintenance service, found health care inaccessible, costly, and complicated—so much so that he was priced out of the market altogether. Says Sammy, "Based on the high costs of health care insurance, it was not feasible for my company to offer health coverage even as a shared expense."

The fact is, if you're not careful, you may indeed lose some or all of the benefits that you depend on when you make the move from a regular career to self-employment. This possibility can be a huge barrier to self-employment; no one wants to put the health and well-being of themselves and their loved ones at risk if they don't have to. Unfortunately, the result is that a lot of people who long to become self-employed end up staying in their unfulfilling, dead-end jobs just so they can retain their health care and other benefits.

Benefits—particularly health care benefits—are very important to many people, and their availability (or lack thereof) is sure to weigh heavily on your own self-employment decision-making process. If benefits are important to you, then the key is to try to retain whatever benefits you already have or to

obtain new benefits at an affordable price as you transition to
your new business.

Aspiring entrepreneurs may
use one of five main benefits
strategies:

> If benefits are important to you, then the key is to try to retain whatever benefits you already have or to obtain new benefits at an affordable price as you transition to your new business.

- *Take your existing benefits along with you when you leave your current job or career.* If you're getting health care and other benefits from your current em-
ployer, you'll be offered the opportunity to continue at
least some of those benefits when you leave. Under
COBRA (an acronym for the Consolidated Omnibus
Budget Reconciliation Act), for example, your health care
benefits are continued (in most but not all states) for eighteen months after you terminate employment, assuming
you keep making payments. The payments are generally at
the same cost as they were with your current employer
(except the employer is no longer paying its share), with
the usual addition of a modest administration charge. If
you don't have other sources available to you through a
spouse, then this approach is often your best bet. But
remember: Every state has its own rules, which sometimes
extend the eighteen months. Be sure to get clear on your
options (through your human resources department)
before you leave your current job, not after.

- *Rely on the benefits that your spouse gets from his or her employer.* If your spouse currently gets benefits through
his or her employer—and your spouse plans to stick with
that job—then you can have access to those benefits, too.

You may, in fact, already be on your spouse's health care policies, which will make your transition to self-employment seamless. If not, it's generally no big deal to be added to a spouse's policies—you'll likely pay an extra charge, but the charge will be far less than any separate policy that you might find on your own. Good news: Benefits are not going to pose much of a barrier at all when you start your new business. You may already be covered! In some states, if you are not married, you may be able to get coverage through your life partner.

- *Lease yourself to obtain group benefits.* You may also use an employee leasing company to lease yourself back to your company and thereby take advantage of the group policy the leasing company uses. SOHO Resource Group, a national organization for independent contractors who do work for corporations, provides a related solution. It incorporates you and redirects your 1099 income into your own profit center within the larger company, enabling you to obtain medical coverage that ranges from comprehensive to economical with pretax dollars. Participation is available only through affiliated companies. You can get more details at SOHO's Web site Inc. (http://soho resourcegroup.com).

- *Buy new benefits.* This is the least preferred route but, if you have no other sources of the health care and other benefits that you need, then you really have no other choice. The problem is that, when you go to a health care insurance company and try to sign up, you're going to find that the plans offered to individuals are generally quite expensive. Moreover, if you have any serious preexisting illnesses or conditions, the prices are going to be even higher. In reality, serious preexisting illnesses usually mean either that you're going to be denied coverage or that your insurer will exclude coverage for that particular illness from your policy. Every state is different—be sure to check with your local heath care insurers, HMOs, PPOs, and the like to see what's available for you.

- *Assume more of the risk yourself.* If you're reasonably healthy, and if your children can manage to avoid major accidents or illness as they grow up, there's no reason you can't set aside a savings fund to pay for your health care and other benefits yourself (the Health Insurance Portability and Accountability Act created tax-deductible medical savings accounts [MSAs] for just this purpose). Along with setting up an MSA, you purchase a catastrophic coverage policy that will pay medical expenses in the event of a major medical problem. The problem with this approach, however, is that there's a gap between what you can deposit in your MSA account tax-free and when the catastrophic coverage kicks in, exposing you to significant out-of-pocket expenditures. If you (or your family) have a major illness or accident, you can quickly burn through thousands of dollars to pay for doctors, hospital stays, medications, ambulances—the whole nine yards. You can pay for your routine medical care yourself, while providing yourself with some measure of security knowing that you won't be bankrupted by an unexpected and large medical expense. Keep in mind, too, that many doctors and dentists will offer discounted consultations and treatment for people who do not have insurance.

Of course, you might be concerned about or interested in other benefits besides health care, including these:

Business property

Disability insurance

REDUCING YOUR BURDEN

As you'll soon find out, business benefits—especially health care benefits—are a very expensive proposition for any business, but especially for small businesses. Here are some tips for reducing the price you pay for your benefits:

- *Join an association.* Many associations offer health care, disability, and life insurance to their members as a benefit of membership. These range from professional organizations (engineers, lawyers, etc.) to chambers of commerce to associations formed specifically to sell insurance to small businesspeople. Beware that while you may assume that group coverage is a better buy, this is not necessarily so as the deal the insurance company has with the association allows the company to rate each member individually. Be sure you compare the prices and coverage offered with other options in your particular area.
- *Look for a group plan.* Group plans—in which you join together with other people into one group for insurance purposes—are generally less expensive than individual plans. In addition, a group plan can't turn you away because of any preexisting conditions that you might

Errors and omissions/product or professional liability

General liability

Partnership

Pension or retirement plans (IRAs or 401[k]s)

Small business

have—that in itself can make all the difference in the world when it comes to your peace of mind. Group plans are increasingly being offered to smaller and smaller groups—including two-person businesses—in California, because state law requires it. If you're also a student, you may be able to get coverage through your college or university.

- *Tweak your plans.* There are many ways to adjust your health insurance and other plans to reduce your out-of-pocket expenses. You can, for example, increase your deductible to a higher dollar amount, or you can reduce your coverage. You can delete people from your plan, or you can pay your premiums on an annual basis (in advance) rather than quarterly or monthly.

- *Find out whether the government will pay your tab.* Depending on your income, your age, and where you live, you may be eligible for federal government–paid benefits plans such as Medicare or Medicaid or similar state plans such as Medi-Cal in California. Be sure to check out your eligibility and options before you shell out a bunch of money for a nongovernment-paid plan.

Vehicle

Workers' compensation

If you are interested in these and other benefits, first check with your employer to see which if any of them can be rolled over to your own business, and then arrange to do just that wherever possible. If you can't take certain benefits along with you, then talk with your own insurance company to see what it offers. Alternatively, you can find lots of information (and very competitive prices) on the Internet.

Our Bias

When it comes to overcoming disabilities, age, youth, addictions, lack of education, single parenthood, and a host of other "real" problems that can get in the way of your dreams of self-employment and independence, we have to admit that we have a bias. It's our belief that if you really, truly want to start the kind of business you've chosen, then you can overcome any obstacle in your way. As we saw in the many examples presented in this chapter, many successful entrepreneurs have overcome incredibly difficult barriers on the road to achieving their goals.

Guess what? You can too! Here are three rules for overcoming your problems:

Rule 1: Use computers and the Internet to your advantage.
Computers and the Internet are opening up tremendous new opportunities for people with disabilities to become self-employed and independent. While many people have a difficult time holding down regular jobs—with their inflexibility, their inaccessible workplaces, and their unsuitable equipment—working for yourself allows you to choose your own schedule, work at home (removing the strain and inconvenience of having to arrange reliable trans port to and from the office), and decide for yourself exactly what kind of work is best for you. Also, using computers and the Internet, anyone—like multiple sclerosis victim Gayle Van Dam, who sells her unique walking sticks and umbrellas around the world through her

www.classycanes.com Web site—can conduct business anyplace he or she wants.

Rule 2: Look at the positives; don't dwell on the negatives. We've all got problems, whether it's going through a particularly nasty divorce, or being a single mom, or not graduating from high school, or being addicted to drugs or alcohol, or any number of other possibilities. While these problems are all very real—and can block your path to self-employment if you allow them to—they can be sidestepped. The key is to stop focusing on these problems, which does nothing but drag you down, and start focusing on the positives that you bring with you to your own business—your talent, your compassion, your desire to deliver the best products or services possible, your values of honesty and fair play, and everything else that is good and decent about you. Consider the story of college dropout Brian Scudamore, who started his $12-million-a-year business with nothing more than an old pickup truck, $700 in cash, a great idea, and a burning desire to be successful.

Rule 3: Build a support group. We all need the love and support of those we care for—it can truly make the difference between success and failure. Figure out who supports you and who is working against you, and spend far more time with the former group than you do with the latter group. And be sure to reach out to new supporters—people who are like-minded or who have already gone through what you are going through.

We hope that in having read this chapter and thought about the stories related here, you now believe that having even very serious problems doesn't mean that you can't reach your dreams. In fact, many people with extremely serious challenges have overcome them, making their dreams of independence reality and finding great success with their own businesses.

From the issues and information in this chapter, identify three things you want or need to do. Write them down in the Personal Action Plan in Appendix A: Take-Off Section, beginning on page 294.

CHAPTER NINE

The Single Most Important Ingredient

Why can't I finish what I start?

How can I avoid putting things off?

Why do I lose interest in my goals after I set them?

What can I do to become less averse to taking risks?

Remember the old saying "Never put off until tomorrow what you can do today"? When it comes to starting your own business, this saying really hits the nail on the head. Your business is going to come to life only if you do the things you need to do to bring it to fruition. If you continue to put off these tasks until tomorrow— you're too busy at work, or your kids need you to pick them up at the mall, or your spouse wants you to watch a popular new television show—then when *will* you ever get around to doing them?

Starting a business takes more than thinking about it, talking about it, or dreaming about it. It takes more than telling your friends that you would like to start your own business some day. It takes more than reading a copy of *Inc.* magazine or *Entrepreneur*. It takes more than reading this book. Starting a business requires *action*—you have to set goals, establish tasks, and then complete them. It's not the size of the goals or the tasks that counts; it's the *doing* that is everything.

> It's not the size of the goals or the tasks that counts; it's the doing that is everything.

This chapter is all about learning to finish what you start, avoiding that insidious dream killer—procrastination—and learning to take risks. These are things that you *must* do to start a successful business. There are no shortcuts, there's no one who can do this for you, and there's no genie in a bottle who is going to magically turn your dreams into reality.

You are in charge, and it will take all of your passion, your excitement, your attention, your commitment, your ingenuity, your dedication, and your courage to breathe life into your dreams of self-employment and independence.

If an inability to finish what you start is getting in the way of your dreams of independence, here's what you can do right now. Don't allow this critical phase of becoming your own boss continue; step your way around this obstacle by asking the following questions:

1. What is the Completion Gene?
2. How can I stop procrastinating?
3. How can I learn to take risks?

Let's go through these questions in detail. By the time you're done with this chapter, you'll see that the key to starting a successful new business is the ability to complete the tasks that lead you to your goals. If you can't seem to finish what you start, once you've read this chapter, you should be well on your way to leaping over this particular barrier and on the path to making your dreams of independence a reality.

Question 1: What Is the Completion Gene?

There is a serious misconception out there when it comes to people who start their own businesses. According to Patrick Von Bargen, executive director of the National Commission on Entrepreneurship, "People think of entrepreneurs—certainly this was true during the Internet boom—as a whiz kid who comes up with a business plan, visits a venture capitalist, and goes for broke. Instead, the typical entrepreneur is someone who has an idea, maintains his day job, and brings his idea through various phases."

What? Aren't entrepreneurs supreme risk takers, ready at a moment's notice to throw caution to the wind and to bet the bank (and the financial well-being of themselves and their loved ones) on an idea—any idea—no matter how loopy it might be?

> The Completion Gene is the habit based on psychological need to follow through on what you start and see it to the end.

Actually, no.

Most entrepreneurs are in reality risk-adverse, and they succeed not because Lady Luck happens to smile on them; they succeed because they have one thing that separates them from the rest of the pack: the Completion Gene. What exactly is the Completion Gene?

The Completion Gene is the habit based on psychological need to follow through on what you start and see it to the end—whether it be preparing a proposal, doing a project for a client, or seeing a business through its up and down cycles. In short, the Completion Gene is what separates successful small business owners from the wannabes, and it's the thing that can have the biggest impact on *your* success as an entrepreneur.

Consider these examples of people who have the Completion Gene:

- While her coworkers kicked back during breaks at Houston, Texas, television station KHWB, Annette Rainesalo was busy getting her new voice-over business—Get Me That Voice, of Stafford, Texas—off the ground. Instead of grabbing a cigarette or a cup of coffee, Annette would make a beeline to her car, where she would work her cell phone lining up clients. And that's not all. During the nine-month period before launching her business, Annette woke up most every morning at 4:00 A.M. to do research about the voice-over business and to call prospective clients. Before long—armed with her extensive research and a growing list of clients—Annette was able to quit her job at the television station and throw herself full-time into her own business. Says Annette, "If I ever planned to be serious, [I knew] I'd have to quit and give this a try. At this point, I have over one hundred clients. I'm voicing just about every day in the week. I found something I love."

- Gerald Ritthaler's dream of turning the lowly yuca plant into a popular American snack has been more than ten years in the making, and the story isn't over yet (an article in *Inc.* magazine termed Ritthaler's company—Ritz Foods International, Inc.—"the world's oldest start-up"). High in carbohydrates and fiber, yuca—also known as cassava—is a starchy staple crop regularly eaten by hundreds of millions of people around the world. Gerald started on this particular path in 1989, when he bought a yuca farm to start research on the best methods of cultivation. Only one problem, says Gerald: "There was no water on the property. There was no water for fifteen to twenty miles. That's where I missed." He tried again the following year, buying a nursery farm to grow seedlings. This time he made sure the farm had water. A couple of years later, Gerald bought a larger plot of land in Venezuela to go into full-scale production of yuca, as well as an abandoned government yuca flour mill. When he finally got around to checking out his new flour mill, he was surprised to find that the equipment wouldn't work. Says Ritz Foods general manager Maria Cristina Gonzalez, "Motors had been stolen. Cables were missing." Then, after buying chip-making machinery in Michigan and having it shipped to his farm in Venezuela, part of the equipment caught on fire and was destroyed. The result? Production of his yuca chips, which was scheduled to start soon after the arrival of the chip-making machinery, was delayed by a year. If that wasn't enough, a drought triggered by the El Niño weather condition took a big bite out of his crop, requiring Gerald to invest even more money in bringing in water. Despite all these challenges, Gerald Ritthaler persevered, and he finally rolled his unique Tropic's Yuca Chips out to the American public in 1999, starting with sales in selected markets in Florida. Has he finally found his own field of dreams? Gerald thinks so. "I'm kind of like that movie where they build a baseball diamond in the cornfield. If you build it, they'll come."

• Although spinning, the stationary bicycle craze that took over more than a few gyms in recent years, is today a household word, that definitely would not have been the case if its creator, Johnny Goldberg of Los Angeles, had given up on his idea before it sparked the imagination of a hungry public. The original idea for spinning—a specially designed, forty-minute bicycling regimen—came to Johnny more than ten years ago. Convinced that his idea was a good one, he opened his own gym in Santa Monica, putting spinning front and center. Unfortunately, the idea didn't catch on, and Johnny was forced to close his gym, moving his equipment (and his classes) to another gym and then, eventually, to his garage. But, despite these setbacks, Johnny refused to give up. With a friend, John Baudhuin, he started Mad Dogg Athletics, Inc., with the goal of popularizing spinning. Mad Dogg Athletics worked with bicycle manufacturer Schwinn to design a new spinning cycle, and Johnny started making the rounds at exercise trade shows. When spinning was named "the hot exercise" in 1994 by *Rolling Stone* magazine, the whole market exploded, and Johnny found himself riding on top of a certified exercise phenomenon. Says John Baudhuin, "Everyone looks at spinning today and says it's a great thing, but back in 1993, we couldn't get anyone but Schwinn to believe in what we were doing. Many companies didn't even want to talk to us."

- Julie Aigner-Clark, whom you met in chapter 5, founded The Baby Einstein Company, a producer of educational videos and flash cards for babies, in 1997. It has since grown into a multimillion-dollar enterprise that was recently acquired by the Disney Company. Success didn't come overnight for Julie, however; it took a lot of hard work and perseverance over a prolonged period. Says Julie, "It took me until my daughter was about eighteen months old to really start to put my ideas into action. I wanted to help mothers (and myself) spend quality time with their babies while exposing them to new cultural, musical, and artistic experiences. So, with no videography experience, I borrowed a friend's video equipment and started filming my first video in the basement of our home. My husband and I financed this project ourselves—it cost about $18,000 to develop, design, and package our first video, money that we took from our savings." Of course, that was just the beginning. Now that Julie had a product, she had to sell it. This took no small amount of work. Says Julie, "Our first big break came when we convinced a baby retailer with about forty-five stores nationally, to test our product on the shelves of six of their stores. The response was amazing. Parents loved the video, and it flew off the shelves, really by word of mouth." As Julie's business began to take off, she found herself stressed (and torn) by the needs of her business and her family. The result? Both get her full attention. According to Julie, "When my company started really growing, I didn't have any help in my house at all. I had the upkeep of my daily life, I had a one-year-old and a three-year-old, and I had my house. So I had to prioritize. The thing I liked to do the least was housework. So I hired someone to help out in the house. That along with my really excellent husband has made all the difference. But I feel like I never really gave up the 'full-time mom stuff'—sometimes it feels so hard to balance. Even now, I feel like I never give either my company or my kids enough attention. It's really a battle when you have your office in your home. On the one hand, I feel really lucky because I can be there, and if my daughter falls down and cries, I can go to her, but it also seems like I work constantly. My day starts at 5:30 A.M., when my kids get up. We usually spend about two hours in the morning just doing stuff together before I even go into my office and start working. But at 10:00 at night, I'm still working—if I walk by my office, I can't resist going to my computer to check my e-mail."

So, what are the key components of the Completion Gene? There are two:

- *Short term: Getting things done.* This is waking up every day and taking steps toward achieving your goals. One day, it may mean buying business cards for your new business, or applying for a business license, or hiring a lawyer to help you incorporate your business. Or it may mean researching your idea on the Internet or calling prospective clients to find out who might be interested in buying the products or services that you intend to offer for sale. You

---

GOAL SETTING AS A JOURNEY

Jennifer Gunnarson, a self-employed acupuncturist and sports therapist in Del Mar, California, looks at achieving one's dreams as a journey, not a destination. While setting goals has been an important element in her own success, Jennifer believes that there's more to completing a task than actually completing it. She says, "I don't think life is about reaching a certain goal and then you're done with that—it's a process. As long as you're sticking to your journey, and you're sticking to your path, and you're trusting your heart, then everything is going to be okay.

"I am not someone who necessarily strictly abides by finishing what I set out to do, because life also has a lot of variances, things happen. One metaphor comes to mind: Say you're doing yoga and you're trying to do a certain pose—you're trying, let's say, to reach your toes. Maybe if you get to your toes, you'll stop there and that will be that—you'll never push yourself to go beyond this particular goal that you set, regardless of the fact that you might be able to achieve far more. So rather than setting

cannot build a business without taking these short-term, but important, steps.

- *Long term: Persistence.* The success of an overnight business is as uncommon as the proverbial three-dollar bill. In reality, the latest craze or hot item is most often the result of *years* of hard work and perseverance. In the prior example of Johnny Goldberg and his spinning craze, it took more than five years from the time he developed the idea until spinning broke onto the national scene in a big way. Johnny could have given up many times along the way, but he didn't, instead pushing his idea until it eventually caught

a goal that is specifically tangible, let it instead be somewhat open-ended.

"Even when I've done personal training," Jennifer continues, "I've never subscribed to the philosophy of 'Let's do three sets of twelve,' because your body doesn't know if it's exhausted at twelve, fifteen, or twenty repetitions. Sometimes, tangible goals can limit you—they put you in a box. Think about how the universe works—it's endless; it just keeps going on and on and on. We can't even see the end. Of course, you have to have small goals to get you to your destination—if you are going to do a marathon, you have to do the training for it. If you're going to start a business, obviously you have to have a business plan and do the preparation. So, if someone wants to work for him- or herself, and he or she has that goal, that's great. Do the things you need to do to get there, but don't set your goal that 'I'm going to have my own business,' because that limits you."

on with the exercising public. You might have the greatest idea since sliced bread, but if you aren't willing or able to hang in with it for the long haul, then you'll potentially miss enjoying the gold at the end of your rainbow.

What Can You Do to Exercise Your Completion Gene?

First, be sure that the business you've decided to start is one that doesn't just promise to pay the bills but inspires you and ignites your passion. When you've found the right business, you'll know it because you'll naturally want to devote as much time as you possibly can to get it off the ground and to make it a success.

Be sure that the business you've decided to start is one that doesn't just promise to pay the bills but inspires you and ignites your passion.

Spend at least twenty hours a week working on your new business if you're currently in a full-time job or career—or more, if you're not. Make a list of all the tasks you need to accomplish to get your business started, and work your way through it, starting at the top and working your way down.

Do something every day that advances your business forward. No matter how small the task, when it's complete, you'll be that much closer to achieving your dreams.

Invite your friends and family to help you. When you ask others to help, you make commitments to them—and they make commitments to you—that will encourage you to keep moving forward with your business. It's harder to put your business aside when others are involved and committed.

Don't let a few nos get you down. Chances are, you're going to run into more than a few of them as you build your business, and it's likely that you'll run into adversity and challenges galore along the way. Throughout it all,

> It's harder to put your business aside when others are involved and committed.

stay positive, and keep moving forward. Be persistent. If you keep a positive attitude and believe in yourself and your idea, you *will* eventually achieve your goals.

You may not think that you were born with the Completion Gene, but, believe us, it's there deep inside you. The Completion Gene is built into each one of us—it's standard equipment from the factory. If you haven't seen your Completion Gene lately, you might need to dust it off before you'll have an opportunity to give it a workout. The more you exercise it, the stronger it will get. And the stronger it gets, the closer you will be to living your dreams instead of just dreaming them.

Key Questions: Do you have the Completion Gene? If you can't seem to find it, what can you do to bring it out? It's there somewhere. Does the business you have chosen to pursue excite you? And not just interest *you, but does it stir your passions and ignite your soul? If not, can you find the business that does? Have you created a list of all the tasks and goals that you'll need to complete to achieve your dreams? If not, why not take some time to do that right now? And, while you're at it, why not commit to dates when you will complete these tasks and goals?*

Question 2: How Can I Stop Procrastinating?

Do you ever think about the things that you put off instead of taking care of immediately—or do you save such thoughts for

POWER OF THE PEN—AND PERSISTENCE

Jodie Lynn of St. Louis, Missouri, writes the syndicated newspaper column "Parent to Parent" and is author of the book *Mommy-CEO*, currently available in a revised edition. She also runs a Web site, www.parenttoparent.com. The path to Jodie's dream of writing her own newspaper column is a case study in perseverance—Jodie clearly has the Completion Gene.

According to Jodie, "I had this idea of possibly writing a family/parenting newspaper column seven years ago. Just getting that idea started was crazy—people would say, 'Oh, you're going to propose to a newspaper that they pick up a column that you've never even written before? Who are you to do this?' But I'm just the kind of person who, if you tell me no, then I do the exact opposite—I get an extreme amount of energy.

"Anyway, I'm a paper person. I love to read the paper and watch *Headline News*—they're my two favorite things. I always noticed that there was very little to zilch in the paper on family and parenting at that time—there was absolutely nothing aside from "Hints from Heloise" and "Dear Abby," and neither wrote about raising kids.

So, I took my idea for a column on parenting to the newspaper and tried to sell them on it. I was turned down because what they wanted me to do was write a column like everyone else did. *That* did not work for me. My idea was unique: that the parents themselves should have the real input into the column, not just me as its author. That was my whole theory. I wanted to give the pat on the back to the parents and the credit to where it should be—with *them*. They could use the column for a nationwide support system and share tried-and-true, real-life parenting challenges. The newspaper didn't really like that concept—it was too revolutionary to have the parents give their input and to take their suggestions literally.

"I just stood my ground and said to the newspaper editor, 'Okay, I'll come up with the proof for it.' So I stood in the mall and talked to strangers about my idea. I asked them, 'What do you think about a newspaper column that would have your input—would you read it? Would that seem like the experts weren't preaching to you, like you had a network system going on sharing ideas on *real* family issues?' Everyone I talked to about my idea loved it. I then interviewed people at parks, restaurants, restrooms—wherever I could—and universally got the same answer, that it was a good idea.

"I went back to the paper and said, 'Okay, now I'm ready to play hardball. I have the information from the public, and it's a go.' The editor said, 'Well, we would rather you tell the parents what to do.' I was very upset, and I was really ready to go to war. So I said, 'Okay, look, you people who are sitting in your ivory towers who don't even know what parenting is, I'm coming in for a meeting—I'll be there Wednesday at 3:00 P.M.' So I showed up Wednesday at 3:00 P.M., and I said, 'I want to know what it is that you don't understand.' I took them by storm—I got them energized. I said, 'Here's who's talking, here's who's reading the papers, here's who will buy the column, and here's why we need it—there's the hole in your newspaper that needs to be filled.' And this time they listened. They agreed to give my column a try. Now it's syndicated through Knight-Ridder/Tribune News Service and available to more than 350 newspapers across the United States and Canada.

"My secret? I just think you have to believe passionately in what you're doing, and that way you will be successful. And even if you get a lot of nos along the way—and there are going to be plenty of them—you turn

(continues)

(continued)

those around into positive energy and say, 'Okay, there's something that I'm not telling these people—let's see what I can do about it.' Another main ingredient in becoming successful is to follow through on what you start. I may take time out to bring my children to practices, attend activities, or volunteer at the school, but I always focus on each project and work diligently until it's completed."

---

sometime *much* later? Procrastination—putting off doing what you should do now until later—is an insidious dream killer, and it can forever keep you from doing what you want to do, when you want to do it. Instead of achieving your dreams, procrastination can keep you from ever reaching them.

Not sure whether you're guilty? Do you ever find yourself thinking or saying any of the following things?

"I'll take care of that tomorrow."

"I'll feel like doing it later."

"There's plenty of time left."

"No problem—I'll be able to get caught up later."

"Let's wait until next week to discuss that."

"I'll have to get back to you later."

"I don't have time to do it right now."

"Can't we wait until next month to set that up?"

The fact is, all of us procrastinate from time to time. It's usually not a problem until we start putting off the things that are most important to us—like pursuing our dreams of self-employment and independence.

Why procrastinate in the first place? Why not just do what you need to do, when you need to do it? There are a variety of possible reasons behind your procrastination; here are some of the more likely possibilities:

You're too tired.

You're bored.

You haven't committed to doing the task.

You have no interest in the outcome.

You lack self-confidence.

You're overwhelmed.

You're afraid you might fail.

You're afraid you might succeed.

Your standards are unreasonably high.

You've taken on too much.

An Exercise in Completion

Ready to exercise your completion muscles? Here are some exercises to help you develop persistence:

1. Make a list of five incomplete things in your life.
2. Complete one.
3. Note how you feel.
4. How can you reward yourself?
5. What does completing mean for your life?

INSIGHTS INTO PROCRASTINATION

Sales expert and motivational speaker Jeffrey Gitomer (www.gitomer.com) knows that procrastinating is a definite obstacle in the path to achieving your goals. In the interview that follows, Jeffrey relates his insights into the downside of procrastination and what to do about it:

Q: Jeffrey, what causes procrastination? Why do people waste time?

A: If you love to do it, you procrastinate less. If people don't see that there's a tremendous reward at the end of their work, there's no major incentive for them to do it. Most people procrastinate (and/or waste time) because they don't like what they do.

There's no passion in it. If you love it, you procrastinate less. Notice I didn't say you don't procrastinate at all; you just tend to procrastinate less. Everyone has some procrastination in them—I don't care who they are.

The rule is: The more you don't like it, the more you procrastinate. When you're procrastinating, you know it.

The other thing is that people tend to have the "moth to a lightbulb" trait in them. Moths don't really care what lightbulb they're going to, just the one that's burning the most brightly. Now that's not only from the standpoint of what is urgent at that moment; it's also what feels good. You may be procrastinating and know it. For example: You have a project that's due, but there's a ball game on, so you watch the ball game first. And you know you're doing it, but the "lightbulb" is on the television and sort of burning brighter, and so you sort of flap your wings around that thing for a while. Then, "I'll just make one sandwich, and then . . . I'll just call this one guy, and then I'm going to go to work. I swear."

Everyone does that. The most interesting thing about procrastination is, when you're doing it, you know it. It's a conscious thing.

Q: Is procrastination a problem or a symptom?

A: Procrastination is a symptom. "I'm a procrastinator" is a symptom. The problem is deeper rooted. Your goals aren't clearly set. You don't really like what you're doing. You're not a well-directed or self-directed person. Those are problems that lead to procrastination.

Q: How do I know whether I have this condition?

A: Look for the early warning signs that cause procrastination:

- You hate your job.
- You are cynical.
- You took a time management course, and it didn't work.
- You lie about lateness.
- You invent excuses similar to "The dog ate my homework."

If you are any of these, you are probably a procrastinator, time waster, or both.

Q: How do I stop wasting time?

A: Set deadlines for achievement. If you write down deadlines for achievement, it helps. Somehow you can always get something done just before the deadline. Here are two things you can do. Number 1 is to set a false (earlier) deadline. Number 2 is to enjoy the deadline instead of lamenting it. How do you enjoy deadlines? You get a positive attitude. You look at it as a learning experience, as opposed to a chore. Even failure is a learning experience. Try to reward yourself with something good after doing something that you don't like.

(continues)

(continued)

Here are some parting thoughts that might create an "A-ha!" about why you procrastinate:

- *Pride in what you do is likely to reduce procrastination.* If you're doing something and you're not proud of the achievement, you're not really looking forward to the achievement. The end result would be "Who cares?" versus "I did it!" For example: You finished your sales report over the weekend so that you could satisfy your boss, whom you hate and don't respect, so you did it on Sunday night watching television and "fudged" a few of the details.
- *If it ain't no fun, do something else.* Do what you love. Money takes care of itself when you do what you love. Challenge: How good of a mood are you in when you come home at night? Bad mood = less likely to achieve.

You're concerned what others will think about your work.

You lack sufficient information.

You lack sufficient training.

You're uncertain what's required.

Your workspace is inadequate.

Key Questions: *If you're a procrastinator, do any of the reasons on the prior list look familiar? If so, which ones? Deal individually with each reason that affects you. If, for example, your workspace is inadequate, then do whatever is necessary*

Here are some more questions to consider:

How often do you tell yourself you can do it later?

How fulfilled are you when you finish projects?

How much do you like and respect your leader at work?

How great do you feel when you get up in the morning?

Reality check: Most people spend more time complaining about their situation than they do solving their situation. If they would just get out of the pity party aspect of their lives and into the solution aspect of their lives, everything would be fine. Productivity (the opposite of procrastination) is a direct result of your desire to produce.

The key to getting anything done is to want to do it.

to bring it up to par. If you lack sufficient training, then figure out where to get the training you need—and then get it! If you're too bored, then find a business that taps into your own natural passion.

So, now that you've seen (and hopefully considered) some of the reasons why you procrastinate instead of taking the actions you need to take to achieve your goals, you might be asking yourself, "Can I change?" We're here to tell you some good news: You *can* change, and you can change right *now*. Don't worry about it being perfect—settle for "good enough." Here are some strategies for overcoming that great, big obstacle in the path to your dreams called procrastination:

- Break your tasks and goals into smaller pieces—they'll be easier to tackle, and you'll have the satisfaction of completing them sooner.
- Get out your camcorder and videotape yourself describing what you plan to do. Studies indicate those who videotape, like those who write things down, are more apt to accomplish their goals.
- Don't beat yourself up for procrastinating—take action instead.
- Reward yourself whenever you complete a task or goal—treat yourself to your favorite snack or take a quick break.

SECRETS OF SUCCESS

Part of avoiding procrastination—and the negative effects it can have on your business-to-be—is to get into a regular work routine. Even if you haven't yet started your business and you're still preparing to get it off the ground, you should act like you're in business. This means having a regular work schedule—just like you do in a regular office. Here are some of our favorite secrets of success:

- *Establish a regular work schedule.* For example, start your workday at 9:00 A.M., and knock off for the day at 3:00 P.M.
- *Schedule a short break once each hour of your workday.* Be sure to recharge your batteries by taking time to eat a healthy lunch!
- *Set up a real office or workspace that is conducive to working and not wasting time.* Avoid having a television or video games (or a bed!) in your office.

- Find a place to work where you'll be free of distractions (friends, kids, television, the Internet, etc.) for a sustained period of time.
- Don't let yourself get too far behind—the farther behind you get, the more difficult it will be to catch up.
- Work on the easiest tasks first.
- Try the ten-minute plan: Work on your least favorite task for ten minutes. At the end of ten minutes, decide whether to continue for ten more minutes or to switch to a different task.
- If you're stuck, change your environment to shake up your thinking. Move to a different room or office, or go outside

- *Establish rituals for beginning and ending your workday.* For example, make a pot of coffee or tea and turn on your computer when you start work, and return your e-mail messages and turn off your computer when you finish.
- *Schedule any meetings or other interruptions in your workday in advance.* These include trips to the office supply superstore, time with clients, and time with friends and family.
- *Minimize trips to the grocery or the kitchen.* Instead, buy a small refrigerator for your office to keep cold drinks and healthy snacks close at hand.

and sit in the sun, or take your work to a coffeehouse or city park.

- Recognize your fears and face up to them.
- Make to-do lists and cross off your tasks and goals as you complete them.

Question 3: How Can I Learn to Take Risks?

A common misconception about entrepreneurs is that they are more willing than most people to take dramatic risks when starting their businesses—to "bet the farm," as it were. Actually, most entrepreneurs are risk-adverse, preferring to do their research and to know exactly what they are getting themselves into before they commit to pursuing a new business.

That said, the simple fact that entrepreneurs are willing to leave behind the security of a regular job or career—with its steady paycheck, company-paid benefits, and other perks—makes them inherently more willing to take risks than the vast majority of people who dream about starting their own businesses, but for one reason or another never actually do it.

> Most entrepreneurs are risk-adverse, preferring to do their research and to know exactly what they are getting themselves into before they commit to pursuing a new business.

But why aren't more people willing to take risks? And why does a failure to take risks become a big roadblock on the way to turning your dreams into reality? Remember Rich Minitir's quote from chapter 7? According to Rich, it isn't just the freedom to succeed that makes America great, it's also the freedom to *fail*. The freedom to succeed—and to fail—is a powerful driver of the American economic engine.

Why, then—if taking risks is what makes our country so great—are so many people afraid to take risks?

Because of a need to be "right"

Because of a fear of rejection

Because of a need for approval by others

Because of a fear of failure

Because of a desire to avoid conflict

Because of a need for security

Because of a desire to maintain the status quo

Because of a fear of change

Because of _____ (fill in your reason here)

In an April 2002 article in *Entrepreneur* magazine, Geoff Williams suggests the following five-step process for taking smart risks instead of stupid ones:

1. *Determine the worst-case consequences of taking the risk.* If you can't live with the consequences, then it's probably a stupid risk, and you need to hatch a contingency plan or retool the risk so the possible catastrophic results can be downgraded to at least just "bad."

2. *Research the risk you want to take as much as possible.* Wise entrepreneurs look—or at least glance—before they leap.

3. *Seek advice.* Try hiring a consultant, discussing the risk with your employees, or talking it over with a friend and getting some feedback.

4. *Ask yourself, "Will I lie awake at night for the next several years, wishing I had taken this risk?"*

5. *Now ask yourself this question: "Is not taking the risk a bigger risk than taking it?"* If the answer is yes, then what are you waiting for?

Key Questions: *What are the fears, concerns, and worries standing between you and your dreams of self-employment and independence? How, when, and why do they have such a powerful influence over you? What can you do to minimize*

DON'T LET WORRIES DERAIL YOUR DREAMS

As a nineteen-year-old student at Georgia Tech University in Atlanta, T. Renee Wilson founded CMG Communications Management Group, a high-tech consulting firm. While she built her firm from nothing to $5 million in annual revenues in just five years, getting there was no bowl of cherries. In fact, at times, Renee's fears threatened to derail her company. But she was able to overcome her worries and stay focused on the task at hand.

"At one point in my business," Renee says, "I allowed worries to overtake me. It wasn't for a long period, but [during that time], I wasn't able to focus—I was unable to complete projects and provide the type of service my clients expected." The problem is that not only can you see that you are consumed with fear, but your clients can see it, too. If you're afraid, you'll also be tentative, reserved, cautious, and perhaps even nervous, confused, or flustered. None of these kinds of behaviors are going to instill much confidence in your abilities as you sell yourself and your company to prospective clients.

Fortunately, Renee discovered a number of different techniques that were instrumental in helping her work through her fears and, ultimately, in

the impact that these fears, concerns, and worries have on you while you replace them with positive feelings, self-confidence, and a willingness to become a risk taker? Why not start exercising your risk-taking muscles right now?

Our Bias

When it comes to starting and running a thriving business, success does not come by chance. You create your own luck and opportunities by working hard, persevering, being persistent,

ensuring her success. At the top of the list is planning. According to Renee, only by planning ahead can you be assured that you will have something to show for your efforts—simply creating a list of tasks or goals, and then checking them off as they are completed, is a very powerful tool for business success. And, as you make progress in your business plans, your worries will by nature decrease. But it's equally important not to take on too many tasks or goals all at one time. Renee explains, "I [used to] have a list of ten things and tried to work on seven of them simultaneously, but it would take me four times as long to complete just one thing. Stick with one task until you're finished, then move on."

And, if there's one thing that Renee has learned, it's that while taking care of business is important—and it will help you worry less as things get more and more under control—you've also got to take care of yourself. "Regardless of how hectic your schedule is," Renee advises, "take time out every day to do something you enjoy, even if it's only for ten or fifteen minutes."

> You create your own luck and opportunities by working hard, persevering, being persistent, finishing what you start, and following through.

finishing what you start, and following through. And you do it by taking action—not by putting tasks and goals off until some future date, or by waiting for someone else to do it for you, or by lacking the courage to take the kind of calculated risks that can push you and your business forward, closer to your objectives.

Here are three rules for putting your own dreams into action:

- *Rule 1: Exercise your Completion Gene.* While you may think that you weren't born with a Completion Gene, we can assure you that you were. The only problem is, if you haven't used it much lately, then it may have gotten a bit rusty over the years. Exercise your Completion Gene—start with small tasks and bring them to successful completion, then add progressively larger and more complex tasks to your repertoire. Before you know it, your Completion Gene will be right up there with the best of them!

- *Rule 2: Get things done, and be persistent.* There are two key components to the Completion Gene: getting things done (short term) and being persistent (long term). It's not enough to have one or the other; you need both to be successful. You can be great at getting things done in the short term, but if you can't shepherd tasks through the long, drawn-out process that may follow, then your venture may ultimately fail. Similarly, if you can't seem to get all the short-term things done that you need to move your enterprise forward, all the persistence in the world will do you little good.

- *Rule 3: Be prepared to take risks.* Life is one big risk, and so is business. Just as you risk your life every time you cross the street, or eat dinner at a restaurant, or hop a transcontinental flight, so, too, do you risk your financial life every time you borrow money to start a new business, commit to delivering products to a client, or branch out into new product lines. Rather than shying away from taking risks, prepare yourself to face them.

From the issues and information in this chapter, identify three things you want or need to do. Write them down in the Personal Action Plan in Appendix A: Take-Off Section, beginning on page 294. These should complete your personal action plan.

AFTERWORD

You've known for a long time that you want to be your own boss. You've played with the idea. You've thought about it. You've probably even taken certain steps toward this important goal in your life. Now you *know* you can do it. Your goals are within your grasp, and you now have specific steps for getting past any obstacles that might come along and try to get in your way.

Now it's time to act. And to keep acting. Taking specific steps—large or small—from your Personal Action Plan every chance you get—daily, weekly, monthly. Holding strong to your intent. Picking up your plans again and again, each time a crisis, a holiday, or any other diversion comes along. Because they will.

Starting a business is a lot like reading a good novel. There are always the inevitable events that come along to cause you to put that novel down . . . for a while. It's the holiday season. Your daughter's wedding. Your wedding. Your birthday. Your kid's birthday. Your vacation. An unexpected 24/7 assignment at the office. You get the flu. Your kids get the flu. The dog gets the flu. The list of possibilities is endless. But, after the event is behind you, you always come back to that novel and read a few more chapters.

These events are *not* setbacks. They are not stumbling blocks. They are simply life. And, as with getting back to a good novel, you simply have to pick up your plans once your life returns to a semblance of normal. So keep your business plans in your face. Your business notes, cards, to-do lists, goals statements, photos, paperwork—you name it. Put the things that represent your progress toward getting your business under way on your nightstand, your desk, the kitchen counter—anyplace where you'll see them daily—so you don't forget them. Whatever you do, don't stash them away in a file drawer somewhere. Keep them out where you will come across them—or even trip over them—constantly!

Remember that this is what you want to do. Remember the feelings that fuel your desire to be your own boss. Remember that you have your Personal Action Plan to turn to and keep adding to as you go along.

Remember that diversions are natural. And most of all, remember that you have the abilities to create the career and life you seek. All the abilities you need to create an independent, self-defined life are inborn, innate qualities that are part of your human heritage. It is in your nature to create. It is in your nature to contribute, to live with purpose, to make a difference. It is in your nature to be free of encumbrances that prevent you from being the fully capable and creative person you are.

Remember, too, people who work for themselves see more of their families, experience less stress, and feel more relaxed, in part because they live with fewer "would haves" and "should haves." They decide the rhythm and pace of their work and how they will do it ethically and qualitatively.

Even if you should not decide at some point to remain in or return to the job world, there's good news waiting. Research shows that self-employment improves one's ability:

- To make things happen
- To create supportive networks of people
- To deal with stressful situations
- To formulate and achieve business goals
- To make decisions

- To identify and find resources
- To manage time
- To perform and utilize the specific skills and know-how of your work

And keep in mind at all times that in a free country, you *are* your own boss. You can choose what you want to do, how you do it, and when you do it. True security lies in knowing and believing in what you can do. This is your life and you can make of it what you will. We look forward to hearing your stories of success in the near future.

Appendix A:
Take-Off Section

PERSONAL ACTION PLAN

Chapter 2: What I need to learn:

1. _____

2. _____

3. _____

Chapter 3: Motivators I need to use:

1. _____

2. _____

3. _____

Chapter 4: Financial things I need to do:

1. _____

2. _____

3. _____

Chapter 5: What I need to get information on:

1. _____

2. _____

3. _____

Chapter 7: Exercises I need to practice:

1. _____

2. _____

3. _____

Chapter 8: Things I need to do:

1. _____

2. _____

3. _____

Chapter 9: Things I need to practice:

1. _____

2. _____

3. _____

Appendix B:
Finding Money to
Start Your Business

☐ Cash settlements from legal actions (e.g., lawsuits, divorce)

☐ Home loans. A home equity loan can come in the form of a line of credit. Any loan secured by your home puts it at risk. Check your current lender or http://quickenloans.quicken.com.

☐ Inheritances—nobody knew your long-lost Uncle Harvey had accumulated so much.

☐ Life insurance policies—borrowing against or cashing out

☐ Reducing the amount withheld from your salary for taxes. This requires changing your W-4 form. We suggest you consult a tax professional before doing this.

☐ Refinancing your home mortgage, enabling you to take money out with the possibility that, with a lower interest rate, your monthly payments will not increase.

☐ Savings and retirement funds. If you're fifty-nine and a half or older, you can withdraw money from your 401(k) without penalty.

❏ Venture capitalists and investment bankers. Check out www.businesspartners.com and www.vfinance.com.

Other People's Money (OPM)

❏ Bank loan partially guaranteed by the Small Business Administration (SBA)—75 to 80 percent—with the bank liable for the remainder of the loan. Accounting for 83 percent of small business loans, these are available for up to $750,000, with twenty-five years to pay back.

❏ Credit cards. An SBA study shows that 28 percent of small companies use business credit cards, and 39 percent use personal credit cards. To find the lowest rates:

- check out CardWeb.com, Inc., P.O. Box 1700, Frederick, MD 21702 (www.cardweb.com); or

- use cards with introductory rates.

❏ Credit union loan—often the best interest rates available

❏ Investors—either from people you know or from strangers or angels. Visit Access to Capital Electronic Network (Ace-Net) at http://ace-net.sr.unh.edu.

❏ Loans from suppliers or colleagues

❏ Loans from relatives or friends—often the easiest to get but risks your personal relationship if you're not able to repay on time or the lender becomes intrusive. To keep the loan on a businesslike basis and to protect the lender tax-wise, put the loan in writing, payable with interest.

Government

❏ Microloan programs—administered by local lenders selected by the Small Business Administration. Loans of up to $35,000 are character-based. Visit www .sbaonline.sba.gov/financing/microparticipants.html, or call (800) 827-5722.

❏ Grants and loans from federal government programs usually administered by the state governments— targeted to people with disabilities, people who live in rural areas, or individuals who are members of a minority group. See the Catalog of Federal Domestic Assistance at www.cfda.gov.

For more information, see chapter 4.

Appendix C:
Places to Check Out
Health Insurance

- COBRA coverage from your last employer
- Employee leasing companies
- Medical savings account (MSA) with a policy covering catastrophic illness
- Small Business Service Bureau—offers 170 plans in fourteen eastern states at (800) 343-0939; www.sbsb.com
- SOHO Resource Group: http://sohoresourcegroup.com; www.workingfromhome.com
- Your spouse's health insurance with his or her employment

**Web Sites That Provide Price Comparisons
If You Need to Buy an Individual Policy**
- www2.accuquote.com; (800) 442-9899
- www.answercenter.com; (888) 222-4115
- www.bestquote.com; (800) 896-8006
- www.eHealthInsurance.com; (800) 977-8860
- www.e-insure.com; (888) 374-7500
- www.insweb.com
- www.moneycentral.msn.com/insure/healthlp.asp
- www.quickquote.com; (800) 867-2404
- www.quotesmith.com; (800) 556-9393

Companies That Rate the Financial Condition of Insurance Companies

- A.M. Best Company—rates almost 1,500 insurers on "financial security" at www.ambest.com
- Fitch Ratings—covers over 220 life and health insurers making up close to 85 percent of the total industry based on assets at www.fitchratings.com
- Moody's Investor Services—rates about 100 insurers on "financial strength" at www.moodys.com
- Standard & Poor's Corporation—rates the "claims-paying ability" of about 250 companies at www2.standardand poors.com/
- Weiss Research—provides safety ratings of more than 1,100 insurers at (800) 289-9222 or www.weissratings.com

Web Site with Links to Insurance Regulators by State

- http://screwedbyinsurance.com—some states show claims complaint experience of companies licensed in their state

For more information on health and other insurance, see chapter 8.

INDEX